The Right to be Lazy

The Right to be Lazy

by Paul Lafargue

Chicago
Charles H. Kerr Publishing Company

The Right to be Lazy: Essays by Paul Lafargue
Edited with a New Introduction by Bernard Marszalek

Copyright © 2011 by Charles H. Kerr Publishing Company & AK Press

ISBN: 978-1-84935-086-0

Library of Congress Control Number: 2011922335

All inquiries:
C.H. Kerr Company
1726 Jarvis Avenue
Chicago, IL 60626
http://www.charleshkerr.com/

The Charles H. Kerr Publishing Company, established in 1886, publishes
books to enrich the lives of all proletarians.

AK Press	AK Press UK
370 Ryan Ave. #100	PO Box 12766
Chico, CA 94612	Edinburgh EH8 9YE
USA	Scotland
www.akpress.org	www.akuk.com
akpress@akpress.org	ak@akdin.demon.co.uk

AK Press is a worker-run, democratically-managed publisher and
distributor of anarchist literature and other mind-altering material.

For more information see http://www.righttobelazy.com

Cover design by Dave Stevenson
Book Design by Jonathan Winston
Text Fonts: Minion and Frutiger

First Printing: February 2011
10 9 8 7 6 5 4 3 2 1

Contents

Introduction: Lafargue for Today

Bernard Marszalek

PREFACE

The Right to be Lazy, according to Derfler, the American historian who wrote the definitive biography of Paul Lafargue, has been translated into more languages and reprinted more often than any other Marxist text, aside from, of course, *The Communist Manifesto.*[1] It seems therefore remarkable that Lafargue remained an obscure historic personage among most socialists throughout the 20th Century. Even more odd, he is essentially a non-person in France – no grand statues, a no boulevards carry his name and no major French biography exist – even though he cofounded the first Marxist party in France, Parti Ouvrier; was elected as the first Marxist member to the French Chamber of Deputies; and applied a Marxist analysis to a wide range of topics fifty years before any other Frenchman.

While Lafargue never publicly identified himself as an anarchist, and in fact actively opposed them most of his life, it is the anarchists, Wobblies and assorted malcontents who circulated *The Right to be Lazy* as an "underground" text for over a hundred years. C. H. Kerr Company, to its credit, translated it and has kept it in print since 1907. This present edition retains the original historical research of Fred Thompson from the 1989 printing, accompanied by additional Lafargue essays and a new introduction that attempts to situate Lafargue's satiric essay at a time, 125 years after it was written, when it will be appreciated for its insights.

Paul Lafargue

Who was Paul Lafargue?

*"… the proletariat, betraying its instincts, despising its historic
mission, has let itself be perverted by the dogma of work."*

Paul Lafargue

Lafargue joked that he was internationalist by blood (Black, Red and
Jewish) before politics. Lafargue's Haitian grandparents contributed
their black, red and Jewish blood to his heritage, and he attributes the
latter to Karl Marx[2]. His grandparents left after the Haitian revolution
in 1804, along with 20,000 other French nationals and their servants,
and settled in eastern Cuba, where they put down roots and created a
prosperous community. Lafargue was born in Santiago de Cuba, the
second largest city in Cuba at that time. When Paul was a child, his
parents permanently relocated, to Bordeaux, a thriving world port in
southwest France.

While educated in France, Lafargue retained his early knowlege of
Spanish, which made possible a politically active year in Spain later in life.
At the lycée in Bordeaux he gained knowledge of English, the language of
the wine merchants whose trade with England dominated the economy.
In the early 1860's he began his medical studies in Toulouse and
became active in student politics. His participation in demonstrations
with a faction of Proudhonists (some suspected he harbored anarchist
sympathies all his life) precipitated his suspension from college for
two years. In response he emigrated to London to continue his studies,
and soon, following the trajectory of many other political émigrés, he
gravitated to Marx's circle drawn to the radicalism of Marx's sociology
and economics.

Lafargue's visits to the Marx's household soon became the pretext for courting Marx's middle daughter Laura. They were married in 1868 and, with Lafargue's schooling completed, moved to Paris. Lafargue attempted to set up a medical practice, but mainly Paul and Laura spent their time agitating for the French section of the International Workingmen's Association (The First International) to repudiate Proudhonism and adopt Marxism. Paul involved himself in organizing amongst the workers and Laura, as she continued to do her entire life, translated English and German texts to aid this endeavor. Within two years their political activities made it imperative for them to move to Bordeaux to escape Napoleon III's repression of working-class agitation in Paris. Their continuing political activity in Bordeaux, mainly in support of the Paris Commune in 1871, resulted in their narrow escape to Spain to avoid arrest by the local police.

Their refuge in Spain lasted a year during which they devoted themselves to expanding the minuscule Marxist movement in opposition to the indigenous anarchism – in this they failed utterly. They returned to London, in 1872, to live for ten years and when an amnesty was granted the Communards, they moved back to Paris. With the general liberalization of the political environment in France, the Lafargues found a more receptive audience for their ideas with the radicalized workers. Their success meant that they were once again under police surveillance, which amounted to more of a nuisance for them than an impediment, however it was a boon for historians since the detailed record of their political activity was retrievable from the archives.

In 1882, Paul Lafargue and Jules Guesde formed the first Marxist party in France, the Parti Ouvrier. The party grew in a short ten years from a few dozen members to sixteen thousand and by the end of the century functioned as a mass party. Historically, the Parti Ouvrier became associated with Guesde, propelled into the spotlight by his oratory skills and organizational acumen, even though Lafargue was his mentor in Marxism and was by far the more intellectually sophisticated. For almost thirty years Lafargue immersed himself in party politics at a time when electoral politicking, anarchists contended, was diversionary: an arena bubbling with grand expectations, all fizzling out in defeats. The Parti Ouvrier over these years swung from revolutionary politics to reformism and back again. Under Marx's, and later Engel's tutelage, Lafargue maintained an emphasis on political, as opposed to economic, organizing until the last years of his life, when he finally recognized the futility of relying on politics to the exclusion of daily-practiced opposition, as occurs in the workplace. In the last years of his life he took the side of the syndicalists against his old comrades in the party.

The Parti Ouvrier introduced Marx's ideas to the French proletariat probably as much through the efforts of the Lafargue's publishing activities as their organizational work with the party. The Lafargues's translation of essays and books by Marx, Engels and German Marxists had an impressive educational value in France, but Marxism was more effectively disseminated with Paul Lafargue's essays and commentaries.

Lafargue accepted the basic premises of Marx's thought: economic determinism, class struggle and the concept of surplus value. Acceptance of these tenets for a critical understanding of capitalism, and how to oppose it, did not transform Lafargue into an evangelist as it did many Marxists. Lafargue understood Marx's intention that his work be used as a "tool" for further research rather than a doctrine to subscribe to. For example, Lafargue extensively studied the massive industrialization of American agriculture, which already threatened European markets in the nineteenth century. He noted that the large land mass in America, coupled with the lack of an exploitable peasant population, demanded machinery production to harvest foodstuffs, which in turn made overproduction cheap, leading to global dumping of US crops.

On a more theoretical level, Lafargue followed Marx and Engels' interest in human origins and the emerging study of traditional societies that became the academic discipline of anthropology. A recently published work in this field, *Ancient Society*, by the American Lewis Morgan, gained their attention because Morgan's theories of societal evolution corresponded with Marx's materialist interpretation of history. Lafargue praised Morgan's work in this area. He adopted Morgan's research into matriarchal origins to support his view that patriarchal, capitalist societies arose in time and so could be changed. Lafargue used these insights and his readings of Vico, the seventeenth century Italian philosopher who wrote on the historic relevance of myths, to draw upon early Greek legends' revelations of matriarchy in the distant past.

Lafargue delved into historic and social studies not as academic exercises, but like his socio-political critique of Proudhon's misogynist legacy, as building blocks towards a comprehensive vision of a new society. Lafargue's sociological essays had a primary goal – to oppose a philistine bourgeois culture by cultivating a theoretical basis for a creative, life-affirming alternative. And Lafargue ventured beyond the terrain of history to formulate a visionary project – he pioneered a new area, Marxist literary criticism. Most of his essays in the field were published in various political journals, in France and Germany; he strove to see his work, however, recognized by established French literary journals, such as La *Nouvelle Revue* and *La Revue Philosophique*, and he was eventually rewarded with editorial acceptance. Lafargue used this establishment exposure to promulgate Marxist interpretations in an arena of mostly puerile bourgeois drivel.

Only after World War I did a European Marxist literary criticism develop. This new genre, of Lafargue's creation, was prompted in 1870 when he attended George Sand's play *L'Autre*. He reviewed the play within the context of the larger social issues of the heroine's plight as a woman in a patriarchical society. Later, in another literary foray, Lafargue scandalized the bourgeoisie, enthralled by Victor Hugo's romanticism, by castigating Hugo who opposed the Paris Commune, as a "reactionary humbug." Lafargue however was less interested in outraging the bourgeoisie than in attacking Hugo because of the train of proletarians who admired him. Literary works and their authors for Lafargue were targets to expose for complicity with tendencies that undermined the project of a democratic society.

Lafargue took a more nuanced view of Emile Zola, especially with *L'Argent's* publication. In Zola he saw a member of the bourgeoisie who questioned its values, but who failed to recognize the role of social forces and leaned too much on fate to determine the route his characters took. Zola introduced the working-class to literature, yet his realism unlike Balzac's was facile. Lafargue wanted novelists to philosophize and plunge the depths of real life as Balzac did. Fifty years later, one of the most highly regarded Marxist literary critics, Georg Lukacs, shared this distinction.

Lafargue amassed a passable appreciation of a vast repertoire of subject areas with which he assaulted bourgeois culture; in many of these forays he brandished an ironic style and wit that had no equal in nineteenth century Europe. *The Sale of an Appetite, The Rights of the Horse* and *The Rights of Man, Pope Pius IX* and *Paradise, The Religion of Capital* are just a few of his essays that prove this point.

The *Right to be Lazy* stands as Paul Lafargue's most devastating assault on the bourgeoisie precisely because it ridicules one of their core beliefs: the work ethic. The assimilation of this pseudo-ethic by the proletariat provided Lafargue the ideal foil for his wit. To value work as a universal good and as a pillar of proletarian morality reveals a politics oblivious to the massively debilitating effects of wage slavery. For the bourgeoisie to see it mocked as a secular devotion devoid of any ethical and aesthetic content shocked and outraged them. And further, to define work as misery to be avoided at all costs, cannot be tolerated, not only by the bosses, but also by those who pretend to defend "The Workers" from a (falsely) perceived slander. We have lost a great deal of revolutionary clarity over the past hundred years due to the hegemony of bourgeois, reactionary ideas. But not totally. *The Right to be Lazy* remains a classic text of resistance that can still be read today with delight.

The Essay

"... to forge a brazen law forbidding any man to work more than three hours a day, the earth, the old earth, trembling with joy would feel a new universe leaping within her."

Paul Lafargue

By ridiculing the work ethic, Lafargue sought to inoculate the emerging French working class against the deleterious effects of assimilating a self-serving bourgeois mentality. He argued against the "right to work" in the most devastating way possible – by employing satire. To his credit, Lafargue instead of supporting leisure as a modest request for a shorter work-day – like the ten-hour day agitated for by the European labor organizations of his time – chose to defend the outrageous concept of laziness. He wanted to warn the French workers of the future hell he foresaw for them as they began moving into the new manufacturing centers under construction in northern France. While living in England he witnessed first hand the devastating misery of the English industrial army barracked in the squalor of polluted cities. He had no reason to believe French capitalism would take another path.

Advocating laziness is more than a rhetorical device to provoke a scandal. In one short phrase Paul Lafargue reversed the perspective on the economic system of exploitation developing, albeit unevenly, throughout Europe. Like the first glance at a film negative, a switch in perspectives reveals a seemingly unknown reality, yet a familiar one. This is not a utopian trope, nor does it refer to false consciousness based on the cultural manipulations of elite "opinion leaders". To reverse perspective is not swallowing the red pill to reveal the *Matrix* or flying through the magical mirror of *Doctor Parnassus*. To reverse perspective does not open the door to another reality, it questions the one at hand – in this case, a social paradigm that must be interrogated and overcome as an obstacle to our desires.

To reverse perspective on a core belief system of capitalism – that a job satisfies our basic social needs – exposes the ideology of scarcity and sacrifice that supports capitalism's discipline of production. Christian pieties nurture this discipline that courses through the veins of all, even so-called socialists, to promote pride in production, as if toil had value divorced from its content. This absurd belief seeks to justify the contention that workers are entitled to the "fruits of their labor" and juxtaposes the proletariat as heroic producers (of whatever crap) to the capitalists as degenerate idlers and profiteers.

The historic degradation of work, from a pre-capitalist aesthetic of production with roots in traditional societies and their everyday objects of beauty, to a reductionist economic category coincided with the transformation of the crafts person into a factory hand. Technology has but one goal for the capitalist, and that is to reduce the cost of labor. "Labor-saving" mechanization means just that: the capitalist saves the cost of labor by replacing as many workers as possible with machines. As a necessary correlation to this development, labor is de-skilled. Workers as tenders of what Marx called dead labor (machines acquired from the profits of living labor) are therefore not an accidental side effect of capitalism. The transfer of the prideful labor of the skilled crafts persons, internalized as a source of dignity, to the manual labor of the factory hands, that contributes value only for the boss, marks a major ideological triumph of capitalism.

Besides questioning the value of jobs, Lafargue shattered another taboo: time wasted by working. His suggestion that new technologies and managerial efficiencies could reduce the hours of work needs to be seen as an ideological provocation, not a reformist plank in a socialist platform. For the capitalist, the goal of increasing labor productivity is not the reduction of hours to humanize the workplace. More recent investigations into the application of industrial technology show that it supports managers as they structure the organization of work for more control.[3] The enforcement of obedience on the job then becomes the primary reason to introduce technology, with the secondary goal being efficient operation. In other words, non-economic motives determine the length of the workday as it functions as a method of control. If technological innovations did in fact reduce the hours worked, would the workers remain docile? Or would they become emboldened with free time to develop their non-monetized talents and skills away from the job? Better that the chain that binds workers to their tasks is made thicker and stronger by both the length of the working day and the system of abuses the workers endure daily.

Cover of the Solidarity Bookshop
Edition (Chicago, 1969)

The Demise of Work

"A strange delusion possesses the working class . . . this delusion is the love of work, the furious passion for work, pushed even to the exhaustion of the vital force of the individual and his progeny"

Paul Lafargue

The Right to be Lazy, after decades of obscurity, was reprinted by Solidarity Bookshop in the 60's, at a time when academics, hippies and revolutionaries questioned the future of work.[4] The intellectuals fretted over the universal mechanization of manufacturing, exemplified by the automation and robotization of the auto assembly plants. They feared that smart machines would displace millions of skilled workers and threaten future employment prospects of new workers. Given the pivotal role of work to the structure of modern society, these academics sought to accommodate the dislocation they envisioned by proposing reducing hours so that jobs could be shared. They further advocated for policy options to create a leisure society.[5] While they accurately foresaw the decline of manufacturing jobs, their forecast that unemployment would grow to Depression Era proportions proved incorrect. The rise of the service sector and the growth of the prison-industrial-security complex and its spin-off operation the domestic drug trade, coupled with (let us not forget) the government's job program – the military-industrial sector – deflated pleas for full employment, but more importantly it scuttled the prospect of a leisure society that would question, they reasoned, the central role of work in society.

The job market increased beyond all expectations, and yet despite this fact, in the late 60's, many hippies abandoned the increasingly oppressive urban scene and the unappetizing prospect of low paid, boring jobs and retreated to "the land" to do "real work." Some of those who remained in the cities created a proliferation of community-supported collectives and cooperatives. These utopian enterprises were the most practical expression of the quest for authentic work at the time; unfortunately, for various reasons, by the end of the 70's, most collapsed.

The revolutionaries, more precisely those with an anti-authoritarian orientation, investigated the place of work in society by researching historic attempts to institute workers control. They studied the anarchists in Spain in the 30's, the 1956 Workers' Uprising in Hungary, the Italian workers' rebellions in the 70's, and lastly, Solidarnosc, the mass workers' movement in Poland. Solidarnosc, after hundreds of strikes in workplaces throughout Poland, held a congress in September 1981, which issued a call for an economy based on workplace democracy. The congress further proposed a national governing body, like a second parliament, made up exclusively of the working-class. The Poles questioned the nature of work by politicizing it; ironically, recalling hippie pragmatism, the Polish workers' program was the most visionary expression of the quest for authentic work (work that is embedded in a community, not a ruling structure) at the end of the century.

A tiny faction of the 60's revolutionaries questioned the very necessity of work itself and advocated its abolition before the 1968 rebellion of French students and workers inspired many to think of work radically transformed. *The Rebel Worker* Group in Chicago, Fredy Perlman's *Black and Red* and *The Fifth Estate*, both in Michigan, and *Black Mask* in New York City expressed their utter disdain for toil and devised schemes to avoid it. Several dissident intellectuals, like Paul Goodman and Ivan Illich, agreed with these sentiments.

With the rise of temp work agencies in the 80's, a new wave of anti-work rebels appeared. An influx of young people in the job market preferred temporary employment because they had better things to do with their life – continue their education, cultivate artistic talents or involve themselves in political projects. A portion of this temporary work force acquired, early on, technical skills as word processing and computerization entered the office environment. The journal *Processed World*, based in the San Francisco Bay area, arose as a forum for insightful exposés of alienated work and bitter humor written by a cadre of merry office pranksters. In England, *The Idler*, edited by Tom Hodgkinson appeared with a similar outlook and as biting in its satire. When *The Idler* ceased publication, Hodgkinson's Lafargue-like sense of humor resurfaced in his *How to be Idle*, a far more edgy version of Bertrand Russell's *Philosophy of Idleness*, published at the beginning of the twentieth century. Hodgkinson's book was followed a few years later by a French title in the Lafargueian tradition, *Bonjour Laziness: Jumping off the Corporate Ladder*, by Corinne Maier.[6]

These intrusions into the placid terrain of late capitalism's tolerated amusements keep the question of the nature of work before a new generation of wage slaves, who have to cope with the ruinous effects of a system computerizing, outsourcing and speeding up on its way to burnout. Workers today, when they can find jobs, have no option but uncertain employment, since from data entry to college teaching no job is secure. Include non-profits that absorb an idealistic workforce into no-future jobs at starvation wages with no benefits, and this phenomenon, universal in the "developed" world, defines a new labor sector: the precariat – those who submit to precarious employment.

Work has changed dramatically since the nineteenth century, and yet it remains recognizable as enslavement – brutal and crippling, mentally and physically. There is nothing good that can be said for it. Work has been transformed over the decades, however the universal attitudinal and behavioral responses to order-taking, remain unchanged. The pervasive "bad attitude" railed against by capitalists, is sufficient evidence that work as meritorious human activity is discredited for all but the most servile. And when career gurus, without remorse, counsel young people that they will have to "retool" (meaning that they will need to retrain and to commoditize themselves) for six or seven "careers" before they retire, what response can this evoke but utter despair? The work ethic issued from the workers' contractual obligation conceded by them on expectation that the capitalists would guarantee secure and decent employment. For over a hundred years labor struggled to attain this chimeric goal, only to have the bosses methodically trash it in a few decades.

Marx's analysis of the dual nature of work retains its relevance: there is work for profit-making, which we must perform to obtain the means for our individual survival, and there is work, often poorly paid – if paid at all – that serves real needs. In this category we have, for instance, housework, child and eldercare and, of course, that vast expanse of volunteerism millions undertake, mainly as a form of self-administered therapy (to reclaim their humanity), though it is never expressed this way.

Generally unknown are Marx's comments on the worthiness of work itself contained in the last volume of *Capital* (complied by Engels from Marx's notes after he died). There he discusses the "true realm of freedom" beyond "actual material production," unfortunately, Marx left no exegesis on this "true realm of freedom" to serve as a guide to a future beyond work.

Capitalism's singular driving force to maximize financial return through speculation left behind the old industrial economy, the one Marx knew, and hurtled us into an economy barren of work, but not free of it. What we are left with are jobs with a past due shelf life that the desperate seize. Work, in other words, retains its centrality in the lives of people as much by its absence as by its presence. This repetitive pursuit of meaningless work defines the poverty of our lives and the barbarism of capitalism.

If work, as the axis of social relations, becomes an anachronism then how do we define our lives? What becomes our core belief, the motivation to seek activity that both benefits our well-being and that of society? A life of idle pursuits like that of the leisured class is not an option when there is no food on the table. And possibly, no table.

The faint rumblings of discontent with the stresses of American life, in the most part due to the compulsive adherence to the work ethic, have still to cohere into a recognizable opposition. But this much can be said: the demise of work is at hand. The progression of its horror can no longer be ignored. What appeared over two hundred years ago to several poets/ seers, most notably William Blake, as a catastrophe of the human soul has accelerated its pace of destruction. From the specific victims in the early factories, mills and mines – the workers, who could not withstand the relentless grinding of their joints from long hours of toil – the curse of work proceeded to afflict entire families, as young women and children succumbed to the satanic mills. The long hours of work prevented the cultivation of simple garden plots (such as those maintained by the pre-industrial poor) to supplement a meager diet, condemning the factory workers to malnutrition and early death, while industrial pollution adversely affected the health of the nearby communities.

The corporate behemoth continues relentlessly to swell and engorge itself on whole communities, ripping at the fabric of society to conduct its business. Even if labor's role seemed to advance, for instance, at a high-tech facility like Hanford in Washington (admittedly an extreme case, but not unique), the site of the first full-scale plutonium production reactor in the world, they are illusory. Radiation sickness decimated the highly skilled workers despite their promotion by management as the labor force of the future. And here too, the horrors of work extended beyond the technicians and their families to poison nearby communities with radiation. Everyday new reports come from one area of the globe or another that expose a noxious system of production out of control. And now the final descent: the eco-catastrophes of globalization opening the twenty-first century with the prospect that before the century closes, human life, as we know it, will be threatened with extinction.

No place is safe from the relentless pursuit of growth, of capital accumulation propelled by the acquiescence of the exploited who appear to be dedicated to the work ethic, even in the absence of jobs. Posing our situation in that manner is Lafargueian. And it seems obviously wrong-headed, or worse, a slanderous attack on workers. It's blaming the victim, isn't it? Can't work be improved, made safer, and paid better? And what of beneficial public works projects? Everywhere the physical infrastructure collapses, or worse, blows up. That useful work needs to be done is not debatable, however a Lafarguian analysis, precisely because it sees work from the perspective of the worker and not the boss, challenges assumptions about how that work is to be done. To reverse perspective on work challenges those who control it. To assert our desire to break free of the nightmare of a life half lived tied to a job, or longing for one cannot be tolerated by the privileged. It's obvious from the historic record that when the capitalists have been confronted on the nature of the jobs they so generously offer, they resort to violence as their response.

In the nineteen century revolutionaries sought to fight the ravaging beast of capital accumulation by withdrawing work – the General Strike made perfect sense then, and even Lafargue, who originally opposed syndicalism as the false route to power, came round to supporting it late in life. In an age like ours, when the machines of destruction lack safety shut-offs, when the powerlessness of workers is undeniable, how will we stop its rampage? The tactic that comes to mind takes the form of mass desertion, as from war-making. Desertion is a deliberate choice to reassess one's life, a measured response to overcome futility and despair. However, no matter how conscious and rational, to desert is traumatic. The global upheaval gaining momentum precipitates, individually and collectively, an emotional spiral down through self-illusions and social expectations, to our core values. This psychological turbulence historically precedes social change, unfortunately without a guarantee of direction. Is the prospect further enslavement, or liberation?

The forces propelling global transformation one hundred years after Lafargue (he died in 1912) confound easy analysis and remedy. A trinity of devastations – resource depletion, climate change and a failed economy – challenge the notion of sustainable growth as an oxymoron and pose the question of how to scale-down the economy. A mass movement returning "home," may not be on the horizon, but in cities and in rural areas across the world, groups have abandoned the motivation to work that the notion of scarcity compels, to explore a more satisfying way of life, one that defines abundance in qualitative terms. These are the early practitioners of the "true realm of freedom" – the pioneer deserters.

Desertion begins as flight, but with practice, moves to retrieval. By reversing perspective methodically, we gain insight and imagine how to live differently, attuning our desire to live each moment as freely as possible. Stealing time at a job provides that practice, as does sabotage of corporate expectations. However, while individual acts of resistance fortify our resolve, seeking allies based on a shared passion of rebellion is essential. Everything begins with the individual, but nothing ends there[7]. This is not a regimen of grim determination. The aim is to live as Homo Ludens, as depicted in Johan Huizinga's book of that title, which explores the play element of culture. Play as serious pursuits to create a rich source of social aesthetics, such as pursuing games of social re-imagining in actual, tangible, daily life, not as isolated ciphers at computer terminals. Seemingly small and insignificant steps of seizing space – creating communal living spaces, occupying abandoned factory sites to re-industrialize for community use, building a decentralized energy commons, doing spontaneous theater in a bank – are like the late winter blossoms in the field of a new culture, a culture of rhizomic expansion. Development of this sort encourages and connects diverse social projects in a non-hierarchical way to solidify pragmatic politics and to amplify human capabilities that can lead to a truly rich life.

Lafargue's essay implies that to build a new society we need a new foundation for its creation. What is the opposite of work? Neither leisure nor idleness. The opposite of work is autonomous and creative collective activity – ludic activity – that develops our unique humanity and grounds our practice of reversing perspective. The desire to be a jesting whistleblower of daily life's subservience is a revolutionary desire.

---

1 Leslie Derfler, *Paul Lafargue and the Founding of French Marxism* (Harvard, 1991) and *Paul Lafargue and the Flowering of French Socialism* (Harvard, 1998)

2 Daniel De Leon, the leader of the US Socialist Labor Party, reports that when he was touring France and met Lafargue in Lille, in 1904, and asked which of the races that ran

through his veins he had a "predilection for," Paul promptly responded, "I am proudest of my Negro extraction."

3 Stephen A. Marglin, "What Do Bosses Do?" (Part One) *The Review of Radical Political Economics*, Vol.6 No.2; (Part Two) Vol.7 No.1 (1974 & 1975)

4 This edition was designed by Tor Faegre and printed at the J.S. Jordan Memorial Printing Co-op. It was introduced by the following quote from Tristan Tzara:

"Dada demands the introduction of progressive unemployment through comprehensive mechanization of every field of activity. Only by unemployment does it become possible for the individual to achieve certainty as to the truth of life and finally become accustomed to experience."

Solidarity Bookshop was Chicago's anarcho-surrealo-marxist incubator of cultural subversion in the 60's.

5 Robert Theobald, *The Challenge of Abundance* (Clarkson N. Potter, 1961)

6 André Gorz's many books on the subject of work cannot be ignored. Probably the best place to begin is with the posthumous published collection of essays *Ecologica* (Seagull Books 2010)

7 Raoul Vaneigem, *The Revolution of Everyday Life* (PM Press, 2011)

The Right to be Lazy

Paul Lafargue

PREFACE

M. Thiers, at a private session of the commission on primary education of 1849, said: "I wish to make the influence of the clergy all powerful because I count upon it to propagate that good philosophy which teaches man that he is here below to suffer, and not that other philosophy which on the contrary bids man to enjoy." M. Thiers was stating the ethics of the capitalist class, whose fierce egoism and narrow intelligence he incarnated.

The Bourgeoisie, when it was struggling against the nobility sustained by the clergy, hoisted the flag of free thought and atheism; but once triumphant, it changed its tone and manner and today it uses religion to support its economic and political supremacy. In the fifteenth and sixteenth centuries, it had joyfully taken up the pagan tradition and glorified the flesh and its passions, reproved by Christianity; in our days, gorged with goods and with pleasures, it denies the teachings of its thinkers like Rabelais and Diderot, and preaches abstinence to the wage workers. Capitalist ethics, a pitiful parody on Christian ethics, strikes with its anathema the flesh of the laborer; its ideal is to reduce the producer to the smallest number of needs, to suppress his joys and his passions and to condemn him to play the part of a machine turning out work without respite and without thanks.

The revolutionary socialists must take up again the battle fought by the philosophers and pamphleteers of the bourgeoisie; they must march up to the assault of the ethics and the social theories of capitalism;

they must demolish in the heads of the class which they call to action the prejudices sown in them by the ruling class; they must proclaim in the faces of the hypocrites of all ethical systems that the earth shall cease to be the vale of tears for the laborer; that in the communist society of the future, which we shall establish "peaceably if we may, forcibly if we must,"[1] the impulses of men will be given a free rein, for "all these impulses are by nature good, we have nothing to avoid but their misuse and their excesses," and they will not be avoided except by their mutual counter-balancing, by the harmonious development of the human organism, for as Dr. Beddoe says, "It is only when a race reaches its maximum of physical development, that it arrives at its highest point of energy and moral vigor." Such was also the opinion of the great naturalist Charles Darwin.[2]

This refutation of the "Right to Work" which I am republishing with some additional notes appeared in the weekly Egalité, 1880, second series.

Sainte-Pélagie Prison, 1883

---

1. Decartes, *Les Passions de L'âme*
2. Doctor Beddoe, *Memoirs of the Anthropological Society* (In reference to Charles Darwin's *Descent of Man*)

The Right To Be Lazy

*Let us be lazy in everything, except in loving and drinking,
except in being lazy. – Lessing*

Chapter I
A Disastrous Dogma

A strange delusion possesses the working classes of the nations where capitalist civilization holds its sway. This delusion drags in its train the individual and social woes which for two centuries have tortured sad humanity. This delusion is the love of work, the furious passion for work, pushed even to the exhaustion of the vital force of the individual and his progeny. Instead of opposing this mental aberration, the priests, the economists and the moralists have cast a sacred halo over work. Blind and finite men, they have wished to be wiser than their God; weak and contemptible men, they have presumed to rehabilitate what their God had cursed. I, who do not profess to be a Christian, an economist or a moralist, I appeal from their judgement to that of their God; from the preachings of their religious, economics or free thought ethics, to the frightful consequences of work in capitalist society.

In capitalist society work is the cause of all intellectual degeneracy, of all organic deformity. Compare the thorough-bred in Rothschild's stables, served by a retinue of bipeds, with the heavy brute of the Norman farms which plows the earth, carts the manure, hauls the crops. Look at the noble savage whom the missionaries of trade and the traders of religion have not yet corrupted with Christianity, syphilis and the dogma of work, and then look at our miserable slaves of machines.[1]

When, in our civilized Europe, we would find a trace of the native beauty of man, we must go seek it in the nations where economic prejudices have not yet uprooted the hatred of work. Spain, which, alas, is degenerating, may still boast of possessing fewer factories than we have of prisons and barracks; but the artist rejoices in his admiration of the hardy Andalusian, brown as his native chestnuts, straight and flexible as a steel rod; and the heart leaps at hearing the beggar, superbly draped in his ragged *capa*, parleying on terms of equality with the duke of Ossuna. For the Spaniard, in whom the primitive animal has not been atrophied, work is the worst sort of slavery.[2] The Greeks in their era of greatness had only contempt for work: their slaves alone were permitted to labor: the free man knew only exercises for the body and mind. And so it was in this era that men like Aristotle, Phidias, Aristophanes moved and breathed among the people; it was the time when a handful of heroes at Marathon crushed the hordes of Asia, soon to be subdued by Alexander. The philosophers of antiquity taught contempt for work, that degradation of the free man, the poets sang of idleness, that gift from the Gods:

O Melibae Deus nobis haec otia fecit.[3]

Jesus, in his sermon on the Mount, preached idleness: "Consider the lilies of the field, how they grow: they toil not, neither do they spin: and yet I say unto you that even Solomon in all his glory was not arrayed like one of these." Jehovah the bearded and angry god, gave his worshipers the supreme example of ideal laziness; after six days of work, he rests for all eternity.

On the other hand, what are the races for which work is an organic necessity? The Auvergnians; the Scotch, those Auvergnians of the British Isles; the Galicians, those Auvergnians of Spain; the Pomeranians, those Auvergnians of Germany; the Chinese, those Auvergnians of Asia. In our society which are the classes that love work for work's sake? The peasant proprietors, the little shopkeepers; the former bent double over their fields, the latter crouched in their shops, burrow like the mole in his subterranean passage and never stand up to look at nature leisurely. And meanwhile the proletariat, the great class embracing all the producers of civilized nations, the class which in freeing itself will free humanity from servile toil and will make of the human animal a free being – the proletariat, betraying its instincts, despising its historic mission, has let itself be perverted by the dogma of work. Rude and terrible has been its punishment. All its individual and social woes are born of its passion for work.

---

1. European explorers pause in wonder before the physical beauty and the proud bearing of the men of primitive races, not soiled by what Paeppig calls "the poisonous breath of civilization." Speaking of the aborigines of the Oceanic Islands, Lord George Campbell writes: "There is not a people in the world which strikes one more favorably at first sight. Their smooth skin of a light copper tint, their hair golden and curly, their beautiful and happy faces, in a word, their whole person formed a new and splendid specimen of the 'genus homo'; their physical appearance gave the impression of a race superior to ours." The civilized men of ancient Rome, witness Caesar and Tacitus, regarded with the same admiration the Germans of the communist tribes which invaded the Roman empire. Following Tacitus, Salvien, the priest of the fifth century who received the surname of master of the Bishops, held up the barbarians as an example to civilized Christians: "We are immodest before the barbarians, who are more chaste than we. Even more, the barbarians are wounded at our lack of modesty; the Goths do not permit debauchees of their own nation to remain among them; alone in the midst of them, by the sad privilege of their nationality and their name, the Romans have the right to be impure. (Pederasty was then the height of the fashion among both pagans and Christians.) The oppressed fly to the barbarians to seek for mercy and a shelter." (De Gubernatione Dei) The old civilization and the rising Christianity corrupted the barbarians of the ancient world, as the old Christianity and the modern capitalist civilization are corrupting the savages of the new world.

M.F. Leplay, whose talent for observation must be recognized, even if we reject his sociological conclusions, tainted with philanthropic and Christian pharisaism, says in his book *Les Ouvriers Europeans* (1885): "The Propensity of the Bachkirs for laziness (the Bachkirs are semi-nomadic shepherds of the Asiatic slope of the Ural mountains); the leisure of nomadic life, the habit of meditation which this engenders in the best endowed individuals – all this often gives them a distinction of manner, a fineness of intelligence and judgement which is rarely to be observed on the same social level in a more developed civilization ... The thing most repugnant to them is agricultural labor: they will do anything rather than accept the trade of a farmer." Agriculture is in fact the first example of servile labor in the history of man. According to biblical tradition, the first criminal, Cain, is a farmer.

2. The Spanish proverb says: Descanzar es salud. (Rest is healthful.)

3. O Melibaus! A god has granted us this idleness. Virgil, *Bucolics* (See Appendix)

Chapter II
Blessings of Work

In 1770 at London, an anonymous pamphlet appeared under the title, *An Essay on Trade and Commerce*. It made some stir in its time. The author, a great philanthropist, was indignant that "the factory population of England had taken into its head the fixed idea that in their quality of Englishmen all the individuals composing it have by right of birth the privilege of being freer and more independent than the laborers of any country in Europe. This idea may have its usefulness for soldiers, since it stimulates their valor, but the less the factory workers are imbued with it the better for themselves and the state. Laborers ought never to look on themselves as independent of their superiors. It is extremely dangerous to encourage such infatuations in a commercial state like ours, where perhaps seven-eighths of the population have little or no property. The cure will not be complete until our industrial laborers are contented to work six days for the same sum which they now earn in four." Thus, nearly a century before Guizot, work was openly preached in London as a curb to the noble passions of man. "The more my people work, the less vices they will have", wrote Napoleon on May 5th, 1807, from Osterod. "I am the authority ... and I should be disposed to order that on Sunday after the hour of service be past, the shops be opened and the laborers return to their work." To root out laziness and curb the sentiments of pride and independence which arise from it, the author of the *Essay on Trade* proposed to imprison the poor in ideal "work-houses", which should become "houses of terror, where they should work fourteen hours a day in such fashion that when meal time was deducted there should remain twelve hours of work full and complete."

Twelve hours of work a day, that is the ideal of the philanthropists and moralists of the eighteenth century. How have we outdone this *nec plus ultra!* Modern factories have become ideal houses of correction in which the toiling masses are imprisoned, in which they are condemned to compulsory work for twelve or fourteen hours, not the men only but also women and children.[1] And to think that the sons of the heroes of the Terror have allowed themselves to be degraded by the religion of work, to the point of accepting, since 1848, as a revolutionary conquest, the law limiting factory labor to twelve hours. They proclaim as a revolutionary principle the Right to Work. Shame to the French proletariat! Only slaves would have been capable of such baseness. A Greek of the heroic times would have required twenty years of capitalist civilization before he could have conceived such vileness.

And if the miseries of compulsory work and the tortures of hunger have descended upon the proletariat more in number than the locusts of the Bible, it is because the proletariat itself invited them. This work, which in June 1848 the laborers demanded with arms in their hands, this they have imposed on their families; they have delivered up to the barons of industry their wives and children. With their own hands they have demolished their domestic hearths. With their own hands they have dried up the milk of their wives. The unhappy women carrying and nursing their babes have been obliged to go into the mines and factories to bend their backs and exhaust their nerves. With their own hands they have broken the life and the vigor of their children. Shame on the proletarians! Where are those neighborly housewives told of in our fables and in our old tales, bold and frank of speech, lovers of Bacchus? Where are those buxom girls, always on the move, always cooking, always singing, always spreading life, engendering life's joy, giving painless birth to healthy and vigorous children? ... Today we have factory girls and women, pale drooping flowers, with impoverished blood, with disordered stomachs, with languid limbs ... They have never known the pleasure of a healthful passion, nor would they be capable of telling of it merrily! And the children? Twelve hours of work for children! 0, misery. But not all the Jules Simon of the Academy of Moral and Political Science, not all the Germinys of jesuitism, could have invented a vice more degrading to the intelligence of the children, more corrupting of their instincts, more destructive of their organism than work in the vitiated atmosphere of the capitalist factory.

Our epoch has been called the century of work. It is in fact the century of pain, misery and corruption.

And all the while the philosophers, the bourgeois economists – from the painfully confused August Comte to the ludicrously clear Leroy Beaulieu; the people of bourgeois literature – from the quackishly romantic Victor Hugo to the artlessly grotesque Paul de Kock – all have intoned nauseating songs in honor of the god Progress, the eldest son of Work. Listen to them and you would think that happiness was soon to reign over the earth, that its coming was already perceived. They rummaged in the dust of past centuries to bring back feudal miseries to serve as a somber contrast to the delights of the present times. Have they wearied us, these satisfied people, yesterday pensioners at the table of the nobility, today pen-valets of the capitalist class and fatly paid? Have they reckoned us weary of the peasant, such as La Bruyere described him? Well, here is the brilliant picture of proletarian delights in the year of capitalist progress 1840, penned by one of their own men, Dr. Villermé, member of the Institute, the same who in 1848 was a member of that scientific society (Thiers, Cousin, Passy, Blanqui, the academician, were in it), which disseminated among the masses the nonsense of bourgeois economics and ethics.

It is of manufacturing Alsace that Dr. Villermé speaks – the Alsace of Kestner and Dollfus, those flowers of industrial philanthropy and republicanism. But before the doctor raises up before us his picture of proletarian miseries, let us listen to an Alsatian manufacturer, Mr. Th. Mieg, of the house of Dollfus, Mieg & Co., depicting the condition of the old-time artisan: "At Mulhouse fifty years ago (in 1813, when modern mechanical industry was just arising) the laborers were all children of the soil, inhabiting the town and the surrounding villages, and almost all owning a house and often a little field." [2] It was the golden age of the laborer. But at that time Alsatian industry did not deluge the world with its cottons, nor make millionaires out of its Dollfus and Koechlin. But twenty-five years after, when Villermé visited Alsace, the modern Minotaur, the capitalist workshop, had conquered the country; in its insatiable appetite for human labor it had dragged the workmen from their hearths, the better to wring them and press out the labor which they contained. It was by thousands that the workers flocked together at the signal of the steam whistle.

"A great number," says Villermé, "five thousand out of seventeen thousand, were obliged by high rents to lodge in neighboring villages. Some of them lived three or four miles from the factory where they worked."

"At Mulhouse in Dornach, work began at five o'clock in the morning and ended at eight o'clock in the evening, summer and winter. It was a sight to watch them arrive each morning into the city and depart each evening. Among them were a multitude of women, pale, often walking bare-footed through the mud, and who for lack of umbrellas when the rain or snow fell, wore their aprons or skirts turned up over their heads. There was a still larger number of young children, equally dirty, equally pale, covered with rags, greasy from the machine oil which drops on them while they work. They were better protected from the rain because their clothes shed water; but unlike the women just mentioned, they did not carry their day's provisions in a basket, but they carried in their hands or hid under their clothing as best they might, the morsel of bread which must serve them as food until time for them to return home.

Thus to the strain of an insufferably long day – at least fifteen hours – is added for these wretches the fatigue of the painful daily journeys. Consequently they reach home overwhelmed by the need of sleep, and next day they rise before they are completely rested in order to reach the factory by the opening time."

Now, look at the holes in which were packed those who lodge in the town:

"I saw at Mulhouse in Dornach, and the neighboring houses, some of those miserable lodgings where two families slept each in its corner on straw thrown on the floor and kept in its place by two planks ... This wretchedness among the laborers of the cotton industry in the department of the upper Rhine is so extreme that it produces this sad result, that while in the families of the manufacturers, merchants, shop-keepers or factory superintendents, half of the children reach their twenty-first year, this same half ceases to exist before the lapse of two years in the families of weavers and cotton spinners."

Speaking of the labor of the workshop, Villermé adds: "It is not a work, a task, it is a torture and it is inflicted on children of six to eight years. It is this long torture day after day which wastes away the laborers in the cotton spinning factories". And as to the duration of the work Villermé observes, that the convicts in prisons work but ten hours, the slaves in the West Indies work but nine hours, while there existed in France after its Revolution of 1789, which had proclaimed the pompous Rights of Man "factories where the day was sixteen hours, out of which the laborers were allowed only an hour and a half for meals."[3]

What a miserable abortion of the revolutionary principles of the bourgeoisie! What woeful gifts from its god Progress! The philanthropists hail as benefactors of humanity those who having done nothing to become rich, give work to the poor. Far better were it to scatter pestilence and to poison the springs than to erect a capitalist factory in the midst of a rural population. Introduce factory work, and farewell joy, health and liberty; farewell to all that makes life beautiful and worth living.[4]

And the economists go on repeating to the laborers, "Work, to increase social wealth", and nevertheless an economist, Destutt de Tracy, answers: "It is in poor nations that people are comfortable, in rich nations they are ordinarily poor"; and his disciple Cherbuliez continues: "The laborers themselves in cooperating toward the accumulation of productive capital contribute to the event which sooner or later must deprive them of a part of their wages". But deafened and stupefied by their own howlings, the economists answer: "Work, always work, to create your prosperity", and in the name of Christian meekness a priest of the Anglican Church, the Rev. Mr. Townshend, intones: Work, work, night and day. By working you make your poverty increase and your poverty releases us from imposing work upon you by force of law. The legal imposition of work "gives too much trouble, requires too much violence and makes too much noise. Hunger, on the contrary, is not only a pressure which is peaceful, silent and incessant, but as it is the most natural motive for work and industry, it also provokes to the most powerful efforts." Work, work, proletarians, to increase social wealth and your individual poverty; work, work, in order that becoming poorer, you may have more reason to work and become miserable. Such is the inexorable law of capitalist production.

Because, lending ear to the fallacious words of the economists, the proletarians have given themselves up body and soul to the vice of work; they precipitate the whole of society into these industrial crises of over-production which convulse the social organism. Then because there is a plethora of merchandise and a dearth of purchasers, the shops are closed and hunger scourges the working people with its whip of a thousand lashes. The proletarians, brutalized by the dogma of work, not understanding that the over-work which they have inflicted upon themselves during the time of pretended prosperity is the cause of their present misery, do not run to the granaries of wheat and cry: "We are hungry, we wish to eat. True we have not a red cent, but beggars as we are, it is we, nevertheless, who harvested the wheat and gathered the grapes." They do not besiege the warehouse of Bonnet, or Jujurieux, the inventor of industrial convents, and cry out: "M. Bonnet, here are your working women, silk workers, spinners, weavers; they are shivering pitifully under their patched cotton dresses, yet it is they who have spun and woven the silk robes of the fashionable women of all Christendom. The poor creatures working thirteen hours a day had no time to think of their toilet. Now, they are out of work and have time to rustle in the silks they have made. Ever since they lost their milk teeth they have devoted themselves to your fortune and have lived in abstinence. Now they are at leisure and wish to enjoy a little of the fruits of their labor. Come, M. Bonnet, give them your silks, M. Harmel shall furnish his muslins, M. Pouyer-Quertier his calicos, M. Pinet his boots for their dear little feet, cold and damp. Clad from top to toe and gleeful, they will be delightful to look at. Come, no evasions, you are a friend of humanity, are you not, and a Christian into the bargain? Put at the disposal of your working girls the fortune they have built up for you out of their flesh; you want to help business, get your goods into circulation – here are consumers ready at hand. Give them unlimited credit. You are simply compelled to give credit to merchants whom you do not know from Adam or Eve, who have given you nothing, not even a glass of water. Your working women will pay the debt the best they can. If at maturity they let their notes go to protest, and if they have nothing to attach, you can demand that they pay you in prayers. They will send you to paradise better than your black-gowned priests steeped in tobacco."

Instead of taking advantage of periods of crisis, for a general distribution of their products and a universal holiday, the laborers, perishing with hunger, go and beat their heads against the doors of the workshops. With pale faces, emaciated bodies, pitiful speeches they assail the manufacturers: "Good M. Chagot, sweet M. Schneider, give us work, it is not hunger, but the passion for work which torments us." And these wretches, who have scarcely the strength to stand upright, sell twelve and fourteen hours of work twice as cheap as when they had bread on the table. And the philanthropists of industry profit by their lockouts to manufacture at lower cost.

If industrial crises follow periods of overwork as inevitably as night follows day, bringing after them lockouts and poverty without end, they also lead to inevitable bankruptcy. So long as the manufacturer has credit he gives free rein to the rage for work. He borrows, and borrows again, to furnish raw material to his laborers, and goes on producing without considering that the market is becoming satiated and that if his goods don't happen to be sold, his notes will still come due. At his wits' end, he implores the banker; he throws himself at his feet, offering his blood, his honor. "A little gold will do my business better," answers the Rothschild. "You have 20,000 pairs of hose in your warehouse; they are worth 20¢ I will take them at 4¢." The banker gets possession of the goods and sells them at 6¢ or 8¢, and pockets certain frisky dollars which owe nothing to anybody: but the manufacturer has stepped back for a better leap. At last the crash comes and the warehouses disgorge. Then so much merchandise is thrown out of the window that you cannot imagine how it came in by the door. Hundreds of millions are required to figure the value of the goods that are destroyed. In the last century they were burned or thrown into the water.[5]

But before reaching this decision, the manufacturers travel the world over in search of markets for the goods which are heaping up. They force their government to annex Congo, to seize on Tonquin, to batter down the Chinese Wall with cannon shots to make an outlet for their cotton goods. In previous centuries it was a duel to the death between France and England as to which should have the exclusive privilege of selling to America and the Indies. Thousands of young and vigorous men reddened the seas with their blood during the colonial wars of the sixteenth, seventeenth and eighteenth centuries.

There is a surplus of capital as well as of goods. The financiers no longer know where to place it. Then they go among the happy nations who are loafing in the sun smoking cigarettes and they lay down railroads, erect factories and import the curse of work. And this exportation of French capital ends one fine morning in diplomatic complications. In Egypt, for example, France, England and Germany were on the point of hair-pulling to decide which usurers shall be paid first. Or it ends with wars like that in Mexico where French soldiers are sent to play the part of constables to collect bad debts.[6]

These individual and social miseries, however great and innumerable they may be, however eternal they appear, will vanish like hyenas and jackals at the approach of the lion, when the proletariat shall say "I will". But to arrive at the realization of its strength the proletariat must trample under foot the prejudices of Christian ethics, economic ethics and free-thought ethics. It must return to its natural instincts, it must proclaim the Rights of Laziness, a thousand times more noble and more sacred than the anaemic Rights of Man concocted by the metaphysical lawyers of the bourgeois revolution. It must accustom itself to working but three hours a day, reserving the rest of the day and night for leisure and feasting.

Thus far my task has been easy; I have had but to describe real evils well known, alas, by all of us; but to convince the proletariat that the ethics inoculated into it is wicked, that the unbridled work to which it has given itself up for the last hundred years is the most terrible scourge that has ever struck humanity, that work will become a mere condiment to the pleasures of idleness, a beneficial exercise to the human organism, a passion useful to the social organism only when wisely regulated and limited to a maximum of three hours a day; this is an arduous task beyond my strength. Only communist physiologists, hygienists and economists could undertake it. In the following pages I shall merely try to show that given the modern means of production and their unlimited reproductive power it is necessary to curb the extravagant passion of the laborers for work and to oblige them to consume the goods which they produce.

---

1. At the first Congress of Charities held at Brussels in 1857 one of the richest manufacturers of Marquette, near Lille, M. Scrive, to the plaudits of the members of the congress declared with the noble satisfaction of a duty performed: "We have introduced certain methods of diversion for the children. We teach them to sing during their work, also to count while working." That distracts them and makes them accept bravely "those twelve hours of labor which are necessary to procure their means of existence." Twelve hours of labor, and such labor, imposed on children less than twelve years old! The materialists will always regret that there is no hell in which to confine these Christian philanthropic murderers of childhood.

2. Speech delivered before the International Society of Practical Studies in Social Economics, at Paris in May 1863, and published in the *French Economist* .

3. L.R. Villermé. *Tableau de L'état physique et moral des ouvriers dans les fabriques de coton, de laine et de soie* (1840). It is not because Dollfus, Koechlin and other Alsacian manufacturers were republicans, patriots and protestant philanthropists that they treated their laborers in this way, for Blanqui, the academician, Reybaud, the prototype of Jerome Paturot, and Jules Simon have observed the same amenities for the working class among the very catholic and monarchical manufacturers of Lille and Lyons. These are capitalist virtues which harmonize delightfully with all political and religious convictions.

4. The Indians of the warlike tribes of Brazil kill their invalids and old people; they show their affection for them by putting an end to a life which is no longer enlivened by combats, feasts and dances. All primitive peoples have given these proofs of affection to their relatives: the Massagetae of the Caspian Sea (Herodotus), as well as the Wens of Germany and the Celts of Gaul. In the churches of Sweden even lately they preserved clubs called family clubs which served to deliver parents from the sorrows of old age. How degenerate are the modern proletarians to accept with patience the terrible miseries of factory labor!

5. At the Industrial Congress held in Berlin in Jan. 21, 1879 the losses in the iron industry of Germany during the last crisis were estimated at $109,056,000.

6. M. Clemenceau's *Justice* said on April 6. 1880 in its financial department: "We have heard this opinion maintained, that even without pressure the billions of the war of 1870 would have been equally lost for France, that is under the form of loans periodically put out to balance the budgets of foreign countries; this is also our opinion." The loss of English capital on loans of South American Republics is estimated at a billion dollars. The French laborers not only produced the billion dollars paid Bismarck, but they continued to pay interest on the war indemnity to Ollivier, Girardin, Bazaine and other income drawers, who brought on the war and the rout. Nevertheless they still have one shred of consolation: these billions will not bring on a war of reprisal.

Laura in the early 1880's, after
the Lafargues' return to France

Chapter III
The Consequences of Over-Production

A Greek poet of Cicero's time, Antiparos, thus sang of the invention of the water-mill (for grinding grain), which was to free the slave women and bring back the Golden Age: "Spare the arm which turns the mill, Oh, millers, and sleep peacefully. Let the cock warn you in vain that day is breaking. Demeter has imposed upon the nymphs the labor of the slaves, and behold them leaping merrily over the wheel, and behold the axle tree, shaken, turning with it's spokes and making the heavy rolling stone revolve. Let us live the life of our fathers, and let us rejoice in idleness over the gifts that the goddess grants us." Alas! The leisure which the pagan poet announced has not come. The blind, perverse and murderous passion for work transforms the liberating machine into an instrument for the enslavement of free men. Its productiveness impoverishes them.

A good working woman makes with her needles only five meshes a minute, while certain circular knitting machines make 30,000 in the same time. Every minute of the machine is thus equivalent to a hundred hours of the workingwomen's labor, or again, every minute of the machine's labor, gives the working women ten days of rest. What is true for the knitting industry is more or less true for all industries reconstructed by modern machinery. But what do we see? In proportion as the machine is improved and performs man's work with an ever increasing rapidity and exactness, the laborer, instead of prolonging his former rest times, redoubles his ardor, as if he wished to rival the machine. Oh, absurd and murderous competition!

That the competition of man and the machine might have free course, the proletarians have abolished wise laws which limited the labor of the artisans of the ancient guilds; they have suppressed the holidays.[1]

Because the producers of that time worked but five days out of seven, are we to believe the stories told by lying economists that they lived on nothing but air and fresh water? Not so, they had leisure to taste the joys of earth, to make love and to frolic, to banquet joyously in honor of the jovial god of idleness. Gloomy England, immersed in protestantism, was then called "Merrie England." Rabelais, Quevedo, Cervantes, and the unknown authors of the romances make our mouths water with their pictures of those monumental feasts[2] with which the men of that time regaled themselves between two battles and two devastations, in which everything "went by the barrel." Jordaens and the Flemish School have told the story of these feasts in their delightful pictures. Where, Oh, where, are the sublime gargantuan stomachs of those days; where are the sublime brains encircling all human thought? We have indeed grown puny and degenerate. Embalmed beef, potatoes, doctored wine and Prussian schnaps, judiciously combined with compulsory labor have weakened our bodies and narrowed our minds. And the times when man cramps his stomach and the machine enlarges its out-put are the very times when the economists preach to us the Malthusian theory, the religion of abstinence and the dogma of work. Really it would be better to pluck out such tongues and throw them to the dogs.

Because the working class, with its simple good faith, has allowed itself to be thus indoctrinated, because with its native impetuosity it has blindly hurled itself into work and abstinence, the capitalist class has found itself condemned to laziness and forced enjoyment, to unproductiveness and over consumption. But if the over-work of the laborer bruises his flesh and tortures his nerves, it is also fertile in griefs for the capitalist.

The abstinence to which the productive class condemns itself obliges the capitalists to devote themselves to the over-consumption of the products turned out so riotously by the laborers. At the beginning of capitalist production a century or two ago, the capitalist was a steady man of reasonable and peaceable habits. He contented himself with one wife or thereabouts. He drank only when he was thirsty and ate only when he was hungry. He left to the lords and ladies of the court the noble virtues of debauchery. Today every son of the newly rich makes it incumbent upon himself to cultivate the disease for which quicksilver is a specific in order to justify the labors imposed upon the workmen in quicksilver mines; every capitalist crams himself with capons stuffed with truffles and with the choicest brands of wine in order to encourage the breeders of blooded poultry and the growers of Bordelais. In this occupation the organism rapidly becomes shattered, the hair falls out, the gums shrink away from the teeth, the body becomes deformed, the stomach obtrudes abnormally, respiration becomes difficult, the motions become labored, the joints become stiff, the fingers knotted. Others, too feeble in body to endure the fatigues of debauchery, but endowed with the bump of philanthropic discrimination, dry up their brains over political economy, or juridical philosophy in elaborating thick soporific books to employ the leisure hours of compositors and pressmen. The women of fashion live a life of martyrdom, in trying on and showing off the fairy-like toilets which the seamstresses die in making. They shift like shuttles from morning until night from one gown into another. For hours together they give up their hollow heads to the artists in hair, who at any cost insist on assuaging their passion for the construction of false chignons. Bound in their corsets, pinched in their boots, decollette to make a coal-miner blush, they whirl around the whole night through at their charity balls in order to pick up a few cents for poor people – sanctified souls!

To fulfill his double social function of non-producer and over-consumer, the capitalist was not only obliged to violate his modest taste, to lose his laborious habits of two centuries ago and to give himself up to unbounded luxury, spicy indigestibles and syphilitic debauches, but also to withdraw from productive labor an enormous mass of men in order to enlist them as his assistants.

Here are a few figures to prove how colossal is this waste of productive forces. According to the census of 1861, the population of England and Wales comprised 20,066,244 persons, 9,776,259 male and 10,289,965 female. If we deduct those too old or too young to work, the unproductive women, boys and girls, then the "ideological professions," such as governors, policemen, clergy, magistrates, soldiers, prostitutes, artists, scientists, etc., next the people exclusively occupied with eating the labor of others under the form of land-rent, interest, dividends, etc. ... there remains a total of eight million individuals of both sexes and of every age, including the capitalists who function in production, commerce, finance, etc. Out of these eight millions the figures run:

Agricultural laborers, including herdsmen, servants and farmers' daughters living at home –1,098,261
Factory Workers in cotton, wool, hemp, linen silk, knitting– 642,607
Mine Workers – 565,835
Metal Workers (blast furnaces, rolling mills, etc.) – 396,998
Domestics – 1,208,648

"If we add together the textile workers and the miners, we obtain the figures of 1,208,442; if to the former we add the metal workers, we have a total of 1,039,605 persons; that is to say, in each case a number below that of the modern domestic slaves. Behold the magnificent result of the capitalist exploitation of machines."[3] To this class of domestics, the size of which indicates the stage attained by capitalist civilization, must still be added the enormous class of unfortunates devoted exclusively to satisfying the vain and expensive tastes of the rich classes: diamond cutters, lace-makers, embroiderers, binders of luxurious books, seamstresses employed on expensive gowns decorators of villas, etc.[4]

Once settled down into absolute laziness and demoralized by enforced enjoyment, the capitalist class in spite of the injury involved in its new kind of life, adapted itself to it. Soon it began to look upon any change with horror. The sight of the miserable conditions of life resignedly accepted by the working class and the sight of the organic degradation engendered by the depraved passion for work increased its aversion for all compulsory labor and all restrictions of its pleasures. It is precisely at that time that, without taking into account the demoralization which the capitalist class had imposed upon itself as a social duty, the proletarians took it into their heads to inflict work on the capitalists. Artless as they were, they took seriously the theories of work proclaimed by the economists and moralists, and girded up their loins to inflict the practice of these theories upon the capitalists. The proletariat hoisted the banner, "He who will not work, neither shall he eat." Lyons in 1831 rose up for bullets or work. The federated laborers of March 1871 called their uprising "The Revolution of Work." To these outbreaks of barbarous fury destructive of all capitalist joy and laziness, the capitalists had no other answer than ferocious repression, but they know that if they have been able to repress these revolutionary explosions, they have not drowned in the blood of these gigantic massacres the absurd idea of the proletariat wishing to inflict work upon the idle and reputable classes, and it is to avert this misfortune that they surround themselves with guards, policemen, magistrates and jailors, supported in laborious unprodutiveness. There is no more room for illusion as to the function of modern armies. They are permanently maintained only to suppress the "enemy within." Thus the forts of Paris and Lyons have not been built to defend the city against the foreigner, but to crush it in case of revolt. And if an unanswerable example be called for, we mention the army of Belgium, that paradise of capitalism. Its neutrality is guaranteed by the European powers, and nevertheless its army is one of the strongest in proportion to its population. The glorious battlefields of the brave Belgian army are the plains of the Borinage and of Charleroi. It is in the blood of the unarmed miners and laborers that the Belgian officers temper their swords and win their epaulets. The nations of Europe have not national armies but mercenary armies. They protect the capitalists against the popular fury which would condemn them to ten hours of mining or spinning. Again, while compressing its own stomach the working class has developed abnormally the stomach of the capitalist class, condemned to over-consumption.

For alleviation of its painful labor the capitalist class has withdrawn from the working class a mass of men far superior to those still devoted to useful production and has condemned them in their turn to unproductiveness and over-consumption. But this troop of useless mouths in spite of its insatiable voracity, does not suffice to consume all the goods which the laborers, brutalized by the dogma of work, produce like madmen, without wishing to consume them and without even thinking whether people will be found to consume them.

Confronted with this double madness of the laborers killing themselves with over-production and vegetating in abstinence, the great problem of capitalist production is no longer to find producers and to multiply their powers but to discover consumers, to excite their appetites and create in them fictitious needs. Since the European laborers, shivering with cold and hunger, refuse to wear the stuffs they weave, to drink the wines from the vineyards they tend, the poor manufacturers in their goodness of heart must run to the ends of the earth to find people to wear the clothes and drink the wines: Europe exports every year goods amounting to billions of dollars to the four corners of the earth, to nations that have no need of them.[5] But the explored continents are no longer vast enough. Virgin countries are needed. European manufacturers dream night and day of Africa, of a lake in the Saharan desert, of a railroad to the Soudan. They anxiously follow the progress of Livingston, Stanley, Du Chaillu; they listen open-mouthed to the marvelous tales of these brave travelers. What unknown wonders are contained in the "dark continent"! Fields are sown with elephants' teeth, rivers of cocoanut oil are dotted with gold, millions of backsides, as bare as the faces of Dufaure and Girardin, are awaiting cotton goods to teach them decency, and bottles of schnaps and bibles from which they may learn the virtues of civilization.

But all to no purpose: the over-fed capitalist, the servant class greater in numbers than the productive class, the foreign and barbarous nations, gorged with European goods; nothing, nothing can melt away the mountains of products heaped up higher and more enormous than the pyramids of Egypt. The productiveness of European laborers defies all consumption, all waste.

The manufacturers have lost their bearings and know not which way to turn. They can no longer find the raw material to satisfy the lawless depraved passion of their laborers for work. In our woolen districts dirty and half rotten rags are raveled out to use in making certain cloths sold under the name of renaissance, which have about the same durability as the promises made to voters. At Lyons, instead of leaving the silk fiber in its natural simplicity and suppleness, it is loaded down with mineral salts, which while increasing its weight, make it friable and far from durable. All our products are adulterated to aid in their sale and shorten their life. Our epoch will be called the "Age of Adulteration" just as the first epochs of humanity received the names of "The Age of Stone," "The Age of Bronze," from the character of their production. Certain ignorant people accuse our pious manufacturers of fraud, while in reality the thought which animates them is to furnish work to their laborers, who cannot resign themselves to living with their arms folded. These adulterations, whose sole motive is a humanitarian sentiment, but which bring splendid profits to the manufacturers who practice them, if they are disastrous for the quality of the goods, if they are an inexhaustible source of waste in human labor, nevertheless prove the ingenuous philanthropy of the capitalists, and the horrible perversion of the laborers, who to gratify their vice for work oblige the manufacturers to stifle the cries of their conscience and to violate even the laws of commercial honesty.

And nevertheless, in spite of the over-production of goods, in spite of the adulterations in manufacturing, the laborers encumber the market in countless numbers imploring: Work! Work! Their super abundance ought to compel them to bridle their passion; on the contrary it carries it to the point of paroxysm. Let a chance for work present itself, thither they rush; then they demand twelve, fourteen hours to glut their appetite for work, and the next day they are again thrown out on the pavement with no more food for their vice. Every year in all industries lockouts occur with the regularity of the seasons. Over-work, destructive of the organism, is succeeded by absolute rest during two or four months, and when work ceases the pittance ceases. Since the vice of work is diabolically attached to the heart of the laborers, since its requirements stifle all the other instincts of nature, since the quantity of work required by society is necessarily limited by consumption and by the supply of raw materials, why devour in six months the work of a whole year; why not distribute it uniformly over the twelve months and force every workingman to content himself with six or five hours a day throughout the year instead of getting indigestion from twelve hours during six months. Once assured of their daily portion of work, the laborers will no longer be jealous of each other, no longer fight to snatch away work from each other's hands and bread from each other's mouths, and then, not exhausted in body and mind, they will begin to practice the virtues of laziness.

Brutalized by their vice, the laborers have been unable to rise to the conception of this fact, that to have work for all it is necessary to apportion it like water on a ship in distress. Meanwhile certain manufacturers in the name of capitalist exploitation have for a long time demanded a legal limitation of the work day. Before the commission of 1860 on professional education, one of the greatest manufacturers of Alsace, M. Bourcart of Guebwiller, declared: "The day of twelve hours is excessive and ought to be reduced to eleven, while work ought to be stopped at two o'clock on Saturday. I advise the adoption of this measure, although it may appear onerous at first sight. We have tried it in our industrial establishments for four years and find ourselves the better for it, while the average production, far from having diminished, has increased." In his study of machines M.F. Passy quotes the following letter from a great Belgian manufacturer M. Ottevaere: "Our machines, although the same as those of the English spinning mills, do not produce what they ought to produce or what those same machines would produce in England, although the spinners there work two hours a day less. We all work two good hours too much. I am convinced that if we worked only eleven hours instead of thirteen we should have the same product and we should consequently produce more economically." Again, M. Leroy Beaulieu affirms that it is a remark of a great Belgian manufacturer that the weeks in which a holiday falls result in a product not less than ordinary weeks.[6]

An aristocratic government has dared to do what a people, duped in their simplicity by the moralists, never dared. Despising the lofty and moral industrial considerations of the economists, who like the birds of ill omen, croaked that to reduce by one hour the work in factories was to decree the ruin of English industry, the government of England has forbidden by a law strictly enforced to work more than ten hours a day, and as before England remains the first industrial nation of the world.

The experiment tried on so great a scale is on record; the experience of certain intelligent capitalists is on record. They prove beyond a doubt that to strengthen human production it is necessary to reduce the hours of labor and multiply the pay days and feast days, yet the French nation is not convinced. But if the miserable reduction of two hours has increased English production by almost one-third in ten years, what breathless speed would be given to French production by a legal limitation of the working day to three hours. Cannot the laborers understand that by over-working themselves they exhaust their own strength and that of their progeny, that they are used up and long before their time come to be incapable of any work at all, that absorbed and brutalized by this single vice they are no longer men but pieces of men, that they kill within themselves all beautiful faculties, to leave nothing alive and flourishing except the furious madness for work. Like Arcadian parrots, they repeat the lesson of the economist: "Let us work, let us work to increase the national wealth." Oh, idiots, it is because you work too much that the industrial equipment develops slowly. Stop braying and listen to an economist, no other than M.L.Reybaud, whom we were fortunate enough to lose a few months ago. "It is in general by the conditions of hand-work that the revolution in methods of labor is regulated. As long as hand-work furnishes its services at a low price, it is lavished, while efforts are made to economize it when its services become more costly."[7]

To force the capitalists to improve their machines of wood and iron it is necessary to raise wages and diminish the working hours of the machines of flesh and blood. Do you ask for proofs? They can be furnished by the hundreds. In spinning, the self-acting mule was invented and applied at Manchester because the spinners refused to work such long hours as before. In America the machine is invading all branches of farm production, from the making of butter to the weeding of wheat. Why, because the American, free and lazy, would prefer a thousand deaths to the bovine life of the French peasant. Plowing, so painful and so crippling to the laborer in our glorious France, is in the American West an agreeable open-air pastime, which he practices in a sitting posture, smoking his pipe nonchalantly.

---

1. Under the old regime, the laws of the church guaranteed the laborer ninety rest days, fifty-two Sundays and thirty-eight holidays, during which he was strictly forbidden to work. This was the great crime of catholicism, the principal cause of the irreligion of the industrial and commercial bourgeoisie: under the revolution, when once it was in the saddle, it abolished the holidays and replaced the week of seven days by that of ten, in order that the people might no longer have more than one rest day out of the ten. It emancipated the laborers from the yoke of the church in order the better to subjugate them under the yoke of work.

The hatred against the holidays does not appear until the modern industrial and commercial bourgeoisie takes definite form, between the fifteenth and sixteenth centuries. Henry IV asked of the Pope that they be reduced. He refused because "one of the current heresies of the day is regarding feasts" (Letters of Cardinal d'Ossat). But in 1666 Perefixus, archbishop of Paris, suppressed seventeen of them in his diocese. Protestantism, which was the Christian religion adapted to the new industrial and commercial needs of the bourgeoisie, was less solicitous for the people's rest. It dethroned the saints in heaven in order to abolish their feast days on earth. Religious reform and philosophical free thought were but pretexts which permitted the jesuitical and rapacious bourgeoisie to pilfer the feast days of the people.

2. These gigantic feasts lasted for weeks. Don Rodrigo de Lara wins his bride by expelling the Moors from old Calatrava, and the Romancero relates the story:
Les bodas fueron en Burgos
Las tornabodas en Salas:
En bodas y tornabodas
Pasaron siete semanas
Tantas vienen de las gentes
Que no caben por las plazas
(The wedding was at Bourges, the infaring at Salas. In the wedding and the infaring seven weeks were spent. So many people came that the town could not hold them ...) The men of these seven-weeks weddings were the heroic soldiers of the wars of independence.

3. Karl Marx's *Capital*.

4. "The proportion in which the population of the country is employed as domestics in the service of the wealthy class indicates its progress in national wealth and civilization." (R.M. Martin, *Ireland Before and After the Union*, 1818). Gambetta, who has denied that there was a social question ever since he ceased to be the poverty-stricken lawyer of the Cafe Procope, undoubtedly alluded to this ever-increasing domestic class when he announced the advent of new social strata.

5. Two examples: The English government to satisfy the peasants of India, who in spite of the periodical famines desolating their country insist on cultivating poppies instead of rice or wheat, has been obliged to undertake bloody wars in order to impose upon the Chinese Government the free entry of Indian opium. The savages of Polynesia, in spite of the mortality resulting from it, are obliged to clothe themselves in the English fashion in order to consume the products of the Scotch distilleries and the Manchester cotton mills.

6. Paul Leroy-Beaulieu, *La Question Ouvrière au XIX siècle* (1872).

7. Louis Reybaud, *Le coton, son regime, ses problèmes* (1863).

Chapter IV
New Songs to New Music

We have seen that by diminishing the hours of labor new mechanical forces will be conquered for social production. Furthermore, by obliging the laborers to consume their products the army of workers will be immensely increased. The capitalist class once relieved from its function of universal consumer will hasten to dismiss its train of soldiers, magistrates, journalists, procurers, which it has withdrawn from useful labor to help it in consuming and wasting. Then the labor market will overflow. Then will be required an iron law to put a limit on work. It will be impossible to find employment for that swarm of former unproductives, more numerous than insect parasites, and after them must be considered all those who provide for their needs and their vain and expensive tastes. When there are no more lackeys and generals to decorate, no more free and married prostitutes to be covered with laces, no more cannons to bore, no more palaces to build, there will be need of severe laws to compel the working women and working men who have been employed on embroidered laces, iron workings, buildings, to take the hygienic and calisthenic exercises requisite to re-establish their health and improve their race. When once we begin to consume European products at home instead of sending them to the devil, it will be necessary that the sailors, dock handlers and the draymen sit down and learn to twirl their thumbs. The happy Polynesians may then love as they like without fearing the civilized Venus and the sermons of European moralists.

And that is not all: In order to find work for all the non-producers of our present society, in order to leave room for the industrial equipment to go on developing indefinitely, the working class will be compelled, like the capitalist class, to do violence to its taste for abstinence and to develop indefinitely its consuming capacities. Instead of eating an ounce or two of gristly meat once a day, when it eats any, it will eat juicy beefsteaks of a pound or two; instead of drinking moderately of bad wine, it will become more orthodox than the pope and will drink broad and deep bumpers of Bordeaux and Burgundy without commercial baptism and will leave water to the beasts.

The proletarians have taken into their heads to inflict upon the capitalists ten hours of forge and factory; that is their great mistake, because of social antagonisms and civil wars. Work ought to be forbidden and not imposed. The Rothschilds and other capitalists should be allowed to bring testimony to the fact that throughout their whole lives they have been perfect vagabonds, and if they swear they wish to continue to live as perfect vagabonds in spite of the general mania for work, they should be pensioned and should receive every morning at the city hall a five-dollar gold piece for their pocket money. Social discords will vanish. Bond holders and capitalists will be first to rally to the popular party, once convinced that far from wishing them harm, its purpose is rather to relieve them of the labor of over-consumption and waste, with which they have been overwhelmed since their birth. As for the capitalists who are incapable of proving their title to the name of vagabond, they will be allowed to follow their instincts. There are plenty of disgusting occupations in which to place them. Dufaure might be set at cleaning public closets, Gallifet[1] might perform surgical operations on diseased horses and hogs. The members of the amnesty commission might be sent to the stockyards to pick out the oxen and the sheep to be slaughtered. The senators might play the part of undertakers and lackeys in funeral processions. As for the others, occupations could be found for them on a level with their intelligence. Lorgeril and Broglie could cork champagne bottles, only they would have to be muzzled as a precaution against intoxication. Ferry, Freycinet and Tirard might destroy the bugs and vermin in the departments of state and other public houses. It would, however, be necessary to put the public funds out of the reach of the capitalists out of due regard for their acquired habits.

But vengeance, harsh and prolonged, will be heaped upon the moralists who have perverted nature, the bigots, the canters, the hypocrites, "and other such sects of men who disguise themselves like maskers to deceive the world. For whilst they give the common people to understand that they are busied about nothing but contemplation and devotion in fastings and maceration of their sensuality – and that only to sustain and aliment the small frailty of their humanity – it is so far otherwise that on the contrary, God knows, what cheer they make; *et Curies simulant, sed Bacchanalia vivunt.*[2] You may read it in great letters, in the coloring of their red snouts, and gulching bellies as big as a tun, unless it be when they perfume themselves with sulphur."[3] On the days of great popular rejoicing, when instead of swallowing dust as on the 15th of August and 14th of July under capitalism, the communists and collectivists will eat, drink and dance to their hearts' content; the members of the Academy, of moral and political sciences; the priests with long robes and short, of the economic, catholic, protestant, jewish, positivist and free-thought church; the propagandists of Malthusianism, and of Christian, altruistic, independent or dependent ethics, clothed in yellow, shall be compelled to hold a candle until it bums their fingers, shall starve in sight of tables loaded with meats, fruits and flowers and shall agonize with thirst in sight of flowing hogsheads. Four times a year with the changing seasons they shall be shut up like the knife grinders' dogs in great wheels and condemned to grind wind for ten hours.

The lawyers and legislators shall suffer the same punishment. Under the regime of idleness, to kill the time, which kills us second by second, there will be shows and theatrical performances always and always. And here we have the very work for our bourgeois legislators. We shall organize them into traveling companies to go to the fairs and villages, giving legislative exhibitions. The generals in riding boots, their breasts brilliantly decorated with medals and crosses, shall go through the streets and courts levying recruits among the good people. Gambetta and his comrade Cassagnac shall tend door. Cassagnac, in full duelist costume, rolling his eyes and twisting his mustache, spitting out burning tow, shall threaten every one with his father's pistol[4] and sink into a hole as soon as they show him Lullier's portrait. Gambetta will discourse on foreign politics and on little Greece, who makes a doctor of him and would set Europe on fire to pilfer Turkey; on great Russia that stultifies him with the mincemeat she promises to make of Prussia and who would fain see mischief brewing in the west of Europe so as to feather her nest in the east and to strangle nihilism at home; on Mr. Bismark who was good enough to allow him to pronounce himself on the amnesty ... then uncovering his mountainous belly smeared over with red and white and blue, the three national colors, he will beat the tattoo on it, and enumerate the delicate little ortolans, the truffles and the glasses of Margaux and Y'quem that it has gulped down to encourage agriculture, and to keep his electors of Belleville in good spirits.

In the barracks the entertainment will open with the *Electoral Farce.*

In the presence of the voters with wooden heads and asses' ears, the bourgeois candidates, dressed as clowns, will dance the dance of political liberties, wiping themselves fore and aft with their freely promising electoral programs, and talking with tears in their eyes of the miseries of the people and with copper in their voices of the glories of France. Then the heads of the voters will bray solidly in chorus, hi han! hi han!

Then will start the great play, *The Theft of the Nation's Goods.*

Capitalist France, an enormous female, hairy-faced and bald-headed, fat, flabby, puffy and pale, with sunken eyes, sleepy and yawning, is stretching herself out on a velvet couch. At her feet Industrial Capitalism, a gigantic organism of iron, with an ape-like mask, is mechanically devouring men, women and children, whose thrilling and heart-rending cries fill the air; the bank with a marten's muzzle; a hyena's body and harpy-hands, is nimbly flipping coins out of his pocket. Hordes of miserable, emaciated proletarians in rags, escorted by gendarmes with drawn sabers, pursued by furies lashing them with whips of hunger, are bringing to the feet of capitalist France heaps of merchandise, casks of wine, sacks of gold and wheat. Langlois, his nether garment in one hand, the testament of Proudhon in the other and the book of the national budget between his teeth, is encamped at the head of the defenders of national property and is mounting guard. When the laborers, beaten with gun stocks and pricked with bayonets, have laid down their burdens, they are driven away and the door is opened to the manufacturers, merchants and bankers. They hurl themselves pell mell upon the heap, devouring cotton goods, sacks of wheat, ingots of gold, emptying casks of wine. When they have devoured all they can, they sink down, filthy and disgusting objects in their ordure and vomitings. Then the thunder bursts forth, the earth shakes and opens, Historic Destiny arises, with her iron foot she crushes the heads of the capitalists, hiccoughing, staggering, falling, unable to flee. With her broad hand she overthrows capitalist France, astounded and sweating with fear.

If, uprooting from its heart the vice which dominates it and degrades its nature, the working class were to arise in its terrible strength, not to demand the Rights of Man, which are but the rights of capitalist exploitation, not to demand the Right to Work which is but the right to misery, but to forge a brazen law forbidding any man to work more than three hours a day, the earth, the old earth, trembling with joy would feel a new universe leaping within her. But how should we ask a proletariat corrupted by capitalist ethics, to take a manly resolution ...

Like Christ, the doleful personification of ancient slavery, the men, the women and the children of the proletariat have been climbing painfully for a century up the hard Calvary of pain; for a century compulsory toil has broken their bones, bruised their flesh, tortured their nerves; for a century hunger has torn their entrails and their brains. Oh Laziness, have pity on our long misery! Oh Laziness, mother of the arts and noble virtues, be thou the balm of human anguish!

---

1. Gallifet was the general who was directly responsible for the massacre of thousands of French workingmen at the closing days of the Paris Commune.

2. They simulate Curius but live like Bacchanals. (Juvenal.)

3. Rabelais, *Pantagruel*, Book II, Chapter XXXIV. Translation of Urquhart and Motteux.

4. Paul de Cassagnac, like his father Granier, was prominent as a conservative politician, journalist and duelist.

Appendix

Our moralists are very modest people. If they invented the dogma of work, they still have doubts of its efficacy in tranquilizing the soul, rejoicing the spirit, and maintaining the proper functioning of the entrails and other organs. They wish to try its workings on the populace, *in animca vili,* before turning it against the capitalists, to excuse and authorize whose vices is their peculiar mission.

But, you, three-for-a-cent philosophers, why thus cudgel your brains to work out an ethics the practice of which you dare not counsel to your masters? Your dogma of work, of which you are so proud, do you wish to see it scoffed at, dishonored? Let us open the history of ancient peoples and the writings of their philosophers and law givers. "I could not affirm," says the father of history, Herodotus, "whether the Greeks derived from the Egyptians the contempt which they have for work, because I find the same contempt established among the Thracians, the Cythians, the Persians, the Lydians; in a word, because among most barbarians, those who learn mechanical arts and even their children are regarded as the meanest of their citizens. All the Greeks have been nurtured in this principle, particularly the Lacedaemonians."[1]

"At Athens the citizens were veritable nobles who had to concern themselves but with the defense and the administration of the community, like the savage warriors from whom they descended. Since they must thus have all their time free to watch over the interests of the republic, with their mental and bodily strength, they laid all labor upon the slaves. Likewise at Lacedaemon, even the women were not allowed to spin or weave that they might not detract from their nobility."[2]

The Romans recognized but two noble and free professions, agriculture and arms. All the citizens by right lived at the expense of the treasury without being constrained to provide for their living by any of the sordid arts (thus, they designated the trades), which rightfully belonged to slaves. The elder Brutus to arouse the people, accused Tarquin, the tyrant, of the special outrage of having converted free citizens into artisans and masons.[3]

The ancient philosophers had their disputes upon the origin of ideas but they agreed when it came to the abhorrence of work. "Nature," said Plato in his social utopia, his model republic, "Nature has made no shoemaker nor smith. Such occupations degrade the people who exercise them. Vile mercenaries, nameless wretches, who are by their very condition excluded from political rights. As for the merchants accustomed to lying and deceiving, they will be allowed in the city only as a necessary evil. The citizen who shall have degraded himself by the commerce of the shop shall be prosecuted for this offense. If he is convicted, he shall be condemned to a year in prison; the punishment shall be doubled for each repeated offense."[4]

In his *Economics*, Xenophon writes, "The people who give themselves up to manual labor are never promoted to public offices, and with good reason. The greater part of them, condemned to be seated the whole day long, some even to endure the heat of the fire continually, cannot fail to be changed in body, and it is almost inevitable that the mind be affected." "What honorable thing can come out of a shop?" asks Cicero. "What can commerce produce in the way of honor? Everything called shop is unworthy an honorable man. Merchants can gain no profit without lying, and what is more shameful than falsehood? Again, we must regard as something base and vile the trade of those who sell their toil and industry, for whoever gives his labor for money sells himself and puts himself in the rank of slaves."[5]

Proletarians, brutalized by the dogma of work, listen to the voice of these philosophers, which has been concealed from you with jealous care: A citizen who gives his labor for money degrades himself to the rank of slaves, he commits a crime which deserves years of imprisonment.

Christian hypocrisy and capitalist utilitarianism had not perverted these philosophers of the ancient republics. Speaking for free men, they expressed their thought naively. Plato, Aristotle, those intellectual giants, beside whom our latter day philosophers are but pygmies, wish the citizens of their ideal republics to live in the most complete leisure, for as Xenophon observed, "Work takes all the time and with it one has no leisure for the republic and his friends." According to Plutarch, the great claim of Lycurgus, wisest of men, to the admiration of posterity, was that he had granted leisure to the citizens of Sparta by forbidding to them any trade whatever. But our moralists of Christianity and capitalism will answer, "These thinkers and philosophers praised the institution of slavery." Perfectly true, but could it have been otherwise, granted the economic and political conditions of their epoch? War was the normal state of ancient societies. The free man was obliged to devote his time to discussing the affairs of state and watching over its defense. The trades were then too primitive and clumsy for those practicing them to exercise their birth-right of soldier and citizen; thus the philosophers and law-givers, if they wished to have warriors and citizens in their heroic republics, were obliged to tolerate slaves. But do not the moralists and economists of capitalism praise wage labor, the modern slavery; and to what men does the capitalist slavery give leisure? To people like Rothschild, Schneider, and Madame Boucicaut, useless and harmful slaves of their vices and of their domestic servants. "The prejudice of slavery dominated the minds of Pythagoras and Aristotle" – this has been written disdainfully; and yet Aristotle foresaw: "that if every tool could by itself execute its proper function, as the masterpieces of Daedalus moved themselves or as the tripods of Vulcan set themselves spontaneously at their sacred work; if for example the shuttles of the weavers did their own weaving, the foreman of the workshop would have no more need of helpers, nor the master of slaves."

Aristotle's dream is our reality. Our machines, with breath of fire, with limbs of unwearying steel, with fruitfulness, wonderful inexhaustible, accomplish by themselves with docility their sacred labor. And nevertheless the genius of the great philosophers of capitalism remains dominated by the prejudice of the wage system, worst of slaveries. They do not yet understand that the machine is the saviour of humanity, the god who shall redeem man from the sordidae artes and from working for hire, the god who shall give him leisure and liberty.

———————————

1. Herodotus. *Book II.*
2. Biot. *De l'abolition de l'esclavage ancien en Occident,* 1840.
3. Livy, *Book I.*
4. Plato's *Republic,* Book V.
5. Cicero's *De Officilis,* I, 42.

The Rights of the Horse and the Rights of Man

Paul Lafargue

Capitalist Civilization has endowed the wage-worker with the metaphysical Rights of Man, but this is only to rivet him more closely and more firmly to his economic duty.

"I make you free," so speak the Rights of Man to the laborer, "free to earn a wretched living and turn your employer into a millionaire; free to sell him your liberty for a mouthful of bread. He will imprison you ten hours or twelve hours in his workshops; he will not let you go till you are wearied to the marrow of your bones, till you have just enough strength left to gulp down your soup and sink into a heavy sleep. You have but one of your rights that you may not sell, and that is the right to pay taxes."

Progress and Civilization may be hard on wage-working humanity but they have all a mother's tenderness for the animals which stupid bipeds call "lower."

Civilization has especially favored the equine race: it would be too great a task to go through the long list of its benefactions; I will name but a few, of general notoriety, that I may awaken and inflame the passionate desires of the workers, now torpid in their misery.

Horses are divided into distinct classes. The equine aristocracy enjoys so many and so oppressive privileges, that if the human-faced brutes which serve them as jockeys, trainers, stable valets and grooms were not morally degraded to the point of not feeling their shame, they would have rebelled against their lords and masters, whom they rub down, groom, brush and comb, also making their beds, cleaning up their excrements and receiving bites and kicks by way of thanks.

Aristocratic horses, like capitalists, do not work; and when they exercise themselves in the fields they look disdainfully, with a contempt, upon the human animals which plow and seed the lands, mow and rake the meadows, to provide them with oats, clover, timothy and other succulent plants.

These four-footed favorites of Civilization command such social influence that they impose their wills upon the capitalists, their brothers in privilege; they force the loftiest of them to come with their beautiful ladies and take tea in the stables, inhaling the acrid perfumes of their solid and liquid evacuations. And when these lords consent to parade in public, they require from ten to twenty thousand men and women to stack themselves up on uncomfortable seats, under the broiling sun, to admire their exquisitely chiseled forms and their feats of running and leaping. They respect none of the social dignities before which the votaries of the Rights of Man bow in reverence. At Chantilly not long ago one of the favorites for the grand prize launched a kick at the king of Belgium, because it did not like the looks of his head. His royal majesty, who adores horses, murmured an apology and withdrew.

It is fortunate that these horses, who can count more authentic ancestors than the houses of Orleans and Hohenzollern, have not been corrupted by their high social station; had they taken it into their heads to rival the capitalists in aesthetic pretensions, profligate luxury and depraved tastes, such as wearing lace and diamonds, and drinking champagne and Chateau-Margaux, a blacker misery and more overwhelming drudgery would be impending over the class of wage-workers.

Thrice happy is it for proletarian humanity that these equine aristocrats have not taken the fancy of feeding upon human flesh, like the old Bengal tigers which rove around the villages of India to carry off women and children; if unhappily the horses had been man-eaters, the capitalists, who can refuse them nothing, would have built slaughter-houses for wage-workers, where they could carve out and dress boy sirloins, woman hams and girl roasts to satisfy their anthropophagic tastes.

The proletarian horses, not so well endowed, have to work for their peck of oats, but the capitalist class, through deference for the aristocrats of the equine race, concedes to the working horses rights that are far more solid and real than those inscribed in the "Rights of Man." The first of rights, the right to existence, which no civilized society will recognize for laborers, is possessed by horses.

The colt, even before his birth, while still in the fetus state, begins to enjoy the right to existence; his mother, when her pregnancy has scarcely begun, is discharged from all work and sent into the country to fashion the new being in peace and comfort; she remains near him to suckle him and teach him to choose the delicious grasses of the meadow, in which he gambols until he is grown.

The moralists and politicians of the "Rights of Man" think it would be monstrous to grant such rights to the laborers; I raised a tempest in the Chamber of Deputies when I asked that women, two months before and two months after confinement, should have the right and the means to absent themselves from the factory. My proposition upset the ethics of civilization and shook the capitalist order. What an abominable abomination – to demand for babies the rights of colts.

As for the young proletarians, they can scarcely trot on their little toes before they are condemned to hard labor in the prisons of capitalism, while the colts develop freely under kindly Nature; care is taken that they be completely formed before they are set to work and their tasks are proportioned to their strength with a tender care.

This care on the part of the capitalists follows them all through their lives. We may still recall the noble indignation of the bourgeois press when it learned that the omnibus company was using peat and tannery waste in its stalls as a substitute for straw: to think of the unhappy horses having such poor litters! The more delicate souls of the bourgeoisie have in every capitalist country organized societies for the protection of animals, in order to prove that they can not be excited by the fate of the small victims of industry. Schopenhauer, the bourgeois philosopher, in whom was incarnated so perfectly the gross egoism of the philistine, could not hear the cracking of a whip without his heart being torn by it.

This same omnibus company, which works its laborers from fourteen to sixteen hours a day, requires from its dear horses only five to seven hours. It has bought green meadows in which they may recuperate from fatigue or indisposition. Its policy is to expend more for the entertainment of a quadrupled than for paying the wages of a biped. It has never occurred to any legislator nor to any fanatical advocate of the "Rights of Man" to reduce the horse's daily pittance in order to assure him a retreat that would be of service to him only after his death.

The Rights of Horses have not been posted up; they are "unwritten rights," as Socrates called the laws implanted by Nature in the consciousness of all men.

The horse has shown his wisdom in contenting himself with these rights, with no thought of demanding those of the citizen; he has judged that he would have been as stupid as man if he had sacrificed his mess of lentils for the metaphysical banquet of Rights to Revolt, to Equality, to Liberty, and other trivialities which to the proletariat are about as useful as a cautery on a wooden leg.

Civilization, though partial to the equine race, has not shown herself indifferent to the fate of the other animals. Sheep, like canons, pass their days in pleasant and plentiful idleness; they are fed in the stable on barley, lucerne, rutabagas and other roots, raised by wage-workers; shepherds conduct them to feed in fat pastures, and when the sun parches the plain, they are carried to where they can browse on the tender grass of the mountains.

The Church, which has burned her heretics, and regrets that she can not again bring up her faithful sons in the love of "mutton," represents Jesus, under the form of a kind shepherd, bearing upon his shoulders a weary lamb.

True, the love for the ram and the ewe is in the last analysis only the love for the leg of mutton and the cutlet, just as the Liberty of the Rights of Man is nothing but the slavery of the wage-worker, since our jesuitical Civilization always disguises capitalist exploitation in eternal principles and bourgeois egoism in noble sentiments; yet at least the bourgeois tends and fattens the sheep up to the day of the sacrifice, while he seizes the laborer still warm from the workshop and lean from toil to send him to the shambles of Tonquin or Madagascar.

Laborers of all crafts, you who toil so hard to create your poverty in producing the wealth of the capitalists, arise, arise! Since the buffoons of parliament unfurl the Rights of Man, do you boldly demand for yourselves, your wives and your children the Rights of the Horse.

Sale of an Appetite
Paul Lafargue

PREFACE

Some years ago an attendant in the insane asylum at Charenton gave me a manuscript which had been entrusted to him by one of the inmates, who had died in a strait-jacket. Its author, Emile Destouches, the attendant asserted, had never been insane; he had without doubt been committed by the orders of some high official; for, during his captivity, they kept him alone, watched by a special guard, who came from outside.

The three hundred sheets, which the attendant gave me and which I still have, are penciled with a feverish hand, evidently written in haste, in a dimly lighted cell. They contain the story which follows. It seemed to me so strange that till now I have hesitated to publish it. But recent studies of specialists on hypnotism and cerebral dualism have revealed such curious phenomena that all current ideas on consciousness, free will, and even human individuality are thrown into confusion. I think, then, that I shall do a service to physiological science by printing the story of Emile Destouches. I need only mention similar cases reported by Chamisso, Mary Shelley, Hoffman, Balzac and recently Besant and Rice. Physicians should collate and compare these extraordinary facts, stated by trustworthy men, study them, and discover their relations to the miracles of religion, which they rob of their supernatural character.

I have been obliged to decipher, disentangle and harmonize the manuscript, but so far as possible I have respected the form given it by the prisoner – the reader will judge whether I should say the madman – of Charenton. I have put his narrative into the third person, and have suppressed certain pathological descriptions which might prove too realistic for the taste of readers outside the medical profession.

Illustration by Dorothy D. Deene
(from *The Sale of an Appetite*, Kerr, 1904)

PART I

It was in the month of December. It was cold, and Emile Destouches was terribly hungry. The snow whitened the pavements, an icy wind pierced the thickest cloaks and forced the scattered pedestrians to hasten their steps. His face blue, his teeth chattering, and his limbs shivering, Emile stood where he had planted himself before the show-window of a restaurant, brilliantly lighted. A five-foot sturgeon reclined in majesty upon a bed of greens; white and plump pullets, their legs in the air, were innocently exposing their hinder parts; larks, plovers and ortolans were encased in slices of bacon; shining apples and magnificent pears, enveloped in lace paper, were reclining luxuriously in the padding of the hampers. A gigantic pie, flanked with silvery sausages and spotted mortadelles, absorbed his entire attention; the pie was ripped open so as to expose its rosy flesh, veined with fat livers and marbled with truffles. Emile opened wide his gluttonous eyes, and clinched his thirty-two long and sharp teeth.

For three days the unhappy man had eaten nothing, extreme hunger twisted and lacerated his intestines, contracted the muscles of his jaws and filled his mouth with saliva. There he was, motionless, not feeling the cold, petrified at the sight of that divine substance which might appease his hunger, end his sufferings and fill his whole being with earthly delights. A fragile window-pane separated him from the object of his desires. One blow of his fist would have broken the window and put the coveted pie within his grasp; indeed he need only have turned the knob of the door, pushed it, stretched out his arm, to have seized and carried to his mouth the joy of his stomach. Still he stood there, glued to the spot, feasting his eyes and aggravating the hunger of his belly. The coward! The man in a state of nature, the savage, would have eaten, and simply said, I am hungry! But the fear of the policeman, and the dread of the moral indignation of our civilized mobs against every flagrant misdemeanor broke his arms and his legs, paralyzing and stifling the imperious cries of nature. And yet what had the wretched fellow to fear? He was dying of hunger, and to end his torture he was thinking of suicide. "What use to live!—I might find something to eat this evening; but what should I have to fight away hunger tomorrow, the next day, all the days ? Why struggle to live when every reason for living is lost, when life is nothing but misery? Enough of it! Miserable starveling, feast your eyes on your last banquet!"

In his feverish passion, he was talking aloud.

A gentleman of near fifty years, tall and extremely fat, with black beard and hair, a bloated face and an enormous abdomen confined with difficulty in a vast overcoat buttoned with much trouble, observed him attentively. He placed his hand on Emile's shoulder.

"You wish to kill yourself?"

"Yes," he answered mechanically.

"You wish to kill yourself because you are hungry?"

"Yes."

"You are young, well built, you are the man I am looking for; follow me."

Emile believed in a providential savior; he obeyed with alacrity. The unknown entered Vefour's, went up the steps to the parlor floor, settled himself in a private compartment and with a friendly gesture invited the young man to seat himself. A little bread was on the table, the starving man bit into it ravenously.

"A little patience, my friend, be careful of your appetite, that most precious of blessings; wait for the chicken soup."

In a twinkling Emile emptied the plate of soup; the oysters arrived.

"You are murdering yourself, why, it is a shame to eat bread with your oysters; taste them by themselves!"

The fat man took nothing; lost in admiration, he watched, supervised and counseled his guest.

"Be moderate. Do not come back to that quail entree:—save yourself for the roast fowl—remember that the lobster salad is still to come."

Just as a skilful jockey restrains the ardor of his thoroughbred, he tempered the voracity of the young man; he desired by judicious halts and scientific delays to prolong his happiness and make him taste its moments more slowly. Emile made several attempts to thank his singular benefactor.

"Do not distract your appetite by talking; you will not often have it in such good condition; I would give a thousand francs, ten thousand francs, for an appetite as capacious as your. Eating is the supreme duty. All religions make of it a sacred right, the most solemn ceremony of Catholicism is the communion, the mastication of God, the theophagic Eucharist. Eating should always be in a religious silence, that the thought may be entirely concentrated on the act that is being performed. The monks, those sublime masters of the gastronomic art, imposed silence in the refectory."

"Ouf! I can eat no more!—I owe you many thanks."

"Keep them for a better occasion; as I am neither a philanthropic free-thinker nor a charitable Christian, I have nothing to do with your gratitude. You have appeased your belly and regained your ears, now listen to me. When you were gazing at the window display of the restaurant with looks burning enough to melt the fat on the hams, I said to myself with envy, if I only possessed such an appetite! Gold, of which I have more than a Jew, procures pleasures of the intelligence and the senses, but I despise them; appetite is above intelligence, above love. I live only by the belly and for the belly, I enjoy only when I eat or when I drink; the rest is vanity. I am Sch___ , that will inform you that my fortune is stupendous; I do not know the number of my millions; at the age of thirty-two I was a coal and railroad king. I can

intoxicate myself with the kisses of love and the fumes of ambition, I can
gather all the joys of earth, but I despise them all, all, understand? I would
give all the pleasures that men pursue for one of the dinners of my chief
cook, the ingenious and scientific chemist, the only man whom I love and
esteem. If Solomon, whom Jehovah touched with his wisdom, grew weary of
men and of God and satiated with the realities of life and the dreams of his
intellect until he exclaimed, "All is vanity," it is because he had only exhausted
the pleasures of love, the joys of reason and the satisfaction of absolute rule,
while he was ignorant of the supreme delights of the table. What is love?
A miserable and fleeting pleasure; it has scarcely begun, when snap!—it is
shattered, vanished—ended. Compared with this, the joys of the stomach
seem eternal; they last delicious hours. The common herd have been wiser
than Solomon; all nations, the African negro as well as the yellow man of
China, have taken as visible sign of social superiority the expanded belly, the
belly enormous and round like the globe. The capitalist bourgeoisie, the class
which rules the world, the class of which I am one of the high and mighty
representatives, has disemburdened itself of all intellectual and manual
labor to devote itself to the exclusive development of the belly, to create
the race of the Ventripotents. Do you know what is the most remarkable
fact of this century-end, the fact which best characterizes our epoch? It is
neither the discovery of the telephone, nor the invention of dynamite, nor
the insurrection of the Commune, nor the defeat of Sedan; it is that little
medal struck by order of the artists, the men of letters, the journalists, the
philosophers, the scientists, the fine flower of the intellectual and refined
bourgeoisie, to remind the coming centuries that within Paris all besieged,
bombarded, blood-sprinkled, pulsing with battle-fever and crying with
hunger, they, as usual, ate well and drank well; what sublime magnanimity of
soul must have been theirs to rise thus above the miseries and pains which
surround them, that they might fulfill with serenity and freedom of spirit the
first and most important of human functions.[1]

"The Hindus, those masters of abstract metaphysics, arrive at the most
mystical ecstasy through contemplating the navel, the central point of the
human belly. The belly is the true God of humanity; it is for its satisfaction
alone that men plow the earth and sail the seas. The belly is the spring of

human actions always stretched and never broken, it is to gorge it that men transport and bring together in great capitals the products of all climes; its needs and its appetites, numerous, voracious and ever renewed, unite in brotherhood the peoples of the universe. Devil take me, I believe I am making a speech. This subject always lifts me into the ideal. Let us return to' earth. Ah! What a sorry animal is man ! How imperfect, how inferior to the other beasts of the earth; nature has behaved toward him like a stepmother; she has neither given him the interminable gullet of the giraffe, to taste long and slowly the fragrance of wines, nor the hot and insatiable stomach of the duck, to digest always without wearying; she has treated this pretended king of creation more harshly than the intestinal worms, the toenias, those thrice-happy beings which bathe themselves in their nourishing fluid, drinking it in through all their pores and always! Man's stomach is limited, wretchedly limited, and to cap the climax of our miseries, we have eyes larger than our belly. But if my stomach shares the weaknesses of humanity, I can at least extend and reinforce its power by buying the appetite of another, just as my brother capitalists buy the virtue and the conscience of their fellow men. I propose, then, that you sell me your digestive power, as my laborers sell me their muscular powers, my engineers their intellectual powers, my cashiers their honesty and the nurses who care for my children their milk and their maternal cares."

"Is it possible?"

"Perfectly so. You produce and furnish the appetite, I will eat and drink for you and you will be satisfied. The moralists, who are untoward and melancholy bipeds, teach solemnly the contempt of what they call disdainfully the pleasures of the flesh; you are young and simple enough to indulge such scruples. Sell me your appetite, which condemns you to labor and poverty, and you shall have money to pay for the pleasures of which you are now deprived. I will allow you a monthly income of 1,500 francs."

"But—"

"No buts! You don't think that enough? Call it two thousand. Consider that if you reject my offer, you will not know where to sleep this evening or where to get your breakfast tomorrow, and if you agree to the bargain the pretty girls of the boulevard will welcome you to their beds."

Emile's eyes sparkled. "Two thousand francs! Two thousand francs a month, that suits me. What must I do?"

"Sign a contract before a notary. Don't look at me that way; I am not Satan, what the devil!—I am just an ordinary mortal, like you. But no living being possesses my power; my science surpasses that of other men. Not all the power of Napoleon I, nor all the science of Darwin gave them the ability to dine twice a day; I possess this mysterious and precious faculty. The nineteenth century, as was declared by the great philosopher of the bourgeoisie, Auguste Comte, is the century of altruism; never, in fact, at any other epoch, has there been such a complete understanding of how to make use of other people. The exploitation of man by the capitalist is so perfected that the most personal qualities, those most inherent in the individual, have been utilized to the profit of another. For the defense of his property the capitalist no longer depends on his own courage, but upon that of certain proletarians disguised as soldiers; the banker consumes the honesty of his cashier, and the manufacturer the vital force of his workmen, as the debauchees use the sex-nature of the Venuses of the pavement. Nevertheless two faculties have as yet escaped our capitalist altruism, the child-bearing faculty of woman and the digestive faculty; no one has yet been able to transform them into goods that can be bought and sold, as are already the innocence of the virgin, the sanctity of the priest, the conscience of the legislator, the brilliancy of the writer and the intelligence of the chemist. The man who shall work that miracle will be greater than Charlemagne and wiser than Newton; he will be the most beneficent of the benefactors of the poor. Then the rich woman will no longer deform her figure by carrying in her abdomen, through long and painful months, the fruit of her womb; she will deposit her fertilized ovum in the womb of a poor woman, and during the nine months that the one who has sold her womb shall be fattening with the blood of her flesh the fetus of the capitalist's wife, she will have a respite from her poverty; for the first time she will rest herself, eating and drinking to her heart's content. The poor man will no longer have to dread his terrible enemy, hunger; he will cultivate his appetite, which will be the merchandise sought by the millionaire, always in quest of that sovereign good, which Greek philosophy never could discover. What a resource the poor will then have—as for me, I know the useful art of having what I eat digested by another; I shall not reveal that secret until on my death-bed."

"You are joking."

"No, my friend, to have digested by another the meats that my stomach takes is in the last analysis neither more wonderful nor more incomprehensible than to have executed at London or at New York, thanks to the telegraph, the thought that my brain conceives, and at the instant it conceives it. I am so far from joking that here are two thousand francs for the first month.

Sch___ and Destouches proceeded to the office of M. Gabarit, who drew up a paper, scrupulously worded, which the two contracting parties signed and sealed. Emile Destouches sold for five years his appetite in consideration of two thousand francs a month, which Sch___ was to pay him in advance. When the contract was signed, Emile took a drink which plunged him into a deep slumber. He awoke to find himself at a restaurant table sitting in front of two beer schooners and a plump girl who was laughing foolishly that she might show her pretty teeth. He thought he was dreaming; he felt of himself, pinched himself; he rattled in his pocket the pieces of gold he had just received; he was no longer hungry; it had really happened. Only the devil knows where he finished the evening so strangely begun.

---

1. The medal referred to by Sch___ (Destouches never spells out his name) was struck at the Paris mint, in honor of the restaurantkeeper, Paul Brebant. On Its face it reads:
> During the siege of Paris, certain persons, accustomed to meet every fortnight with M. Brebant, never once observed that they were dining in a besieged city of two million souls. 1870-71.
The reverse of the medal read as follows:
> TO MONSIEUR PAUL BREBANT.
> Ernest Renan, Paul de St-Victor,
> M. Berthelot, Ch. Blanc, Scherer, Dumesnil, A Nefftzer, Ch. Edmond, Thurot, Marey, E. de Goncourt, J. Bertrand, Theophile Gautier, A. Hebrard.

PART II

All that is new is beautiful, says the wisdom of the nations. The beginnings of his new existence delighted Emile Destouches; at ten each morning, like a believer visited by the supernatural, he felt descend into his stomach meats and drinks which he neither ate nor drank; he did not perceive their odor nor their flavor, but he was obliged to digest them; his stomach was filled by an operation as mystical as that which fertilized the virgin Mary and gave Joseph a little Jesus.

The repasts which he took through the mouth and gullet of his master who had leased him lasted two hours; with his head heavy and his limbs languid, he slept a part of the day, digesting slowly and painfully the meats and the wines which the other had greedily swallowed. Toward three o'clock he went out for a long walk to revive his gorged belly; this was required of him by one of the clauses of the contract. In the evening his stomach was again filled, and he sank into an ophidian sleep. These heroic repasts were not repugnant to his vigorous peasant's constitution, and between times he caught on the wing the pleasures of which poverty had deprived him; he dressed elegantly and ran around with the girls.

"I am nothing any more but a grubsack," he said to himself, "my life is the life of the geese that are crammed for their fat livers; I do not taste the wines nor the meats which I am compelled to digest for my employer. Bah! The people who have lost their sense of smell are in the same case with me; and then, it will last only five years; during that time of forced labor of the stomach, not only shall I be relieved from the labor of mastication and the degrading concern for bread to be found day by day, but I shall save ten or even twenty thousand francs a year. The laborers who are condemned all their lives to the forced labors of the mine and the work-shop would envy my lot."

Thus he tried to console himself by comparing his labor to that of other wage workers; he said to himself that his servitude was temporary and that when it should be ended, he would have amassed a pretty sum which would enable him to live like a bourgeois, doing nothing.

The open air exercise and the labors of Venus to which he devoted himself did not prevent this systematic stuffing from reacting on his robust health; he grew dyspeptic; his stomach became sluggish, his disposition melancholy. M. Gabarit, at whose office he drew his monthly salary, reproved him sharply, reproaching him for his festive nights in the company of gay girls; venereal excesses, the notary insisted, blunted his appetite and weakened his digestive power which, having been sold, no longer belonged to him; he should consider himself in the position of a farm hand, hired by the year, not allowed to dispose of either his time or his strength at his own fancy, but compelled to regulate them according to the needs of the one who hired him. Emile then thought of marriage and of country life.

"I will hunt, ride horseback, plow my fields; my stomach will regain its former vigor and will endure without weariness the loads imposed upon it by my employer."

He reduced his love passages and redoubled his exercises at the gymnasium; but in proportion as he fortified his stomach and increased its digestive capacity, his employer increased the quantity of victuals which he engulfed.

The notary found a young lady to marry, agreeable in appearance, of a respectable family and with a round dowry. The conditions of the marriage contract having been discussed and fixed, the time came for the official introduction of the betrothed pair to each other. Emile, barbered, brushed and burnished, arrived, radiant with hope; he saw himself a landed proprietor, supervising the cultivation of his fields and the care of his live stock. It was three o'clock when his employer had put into his stomach the last mouthful of his ogre-like breakfast, and according to his custom he should have left his wage-worker time to digest it. But scarcely had Destouches entered the parlor of his future mother-in-law, when he felt his stomach, still overloaded, filling itself anew. His employer had just experienced certain annoyances and was in a murderous temper; to dispel his trouble he sat down at the table and began to eat and drink with fury; the mouthfuls and the bumpers that he engulfed were enormous, and succeeded each other without respite. Poor Emile could do no more; the walls of his stomach were distended to bursting; he sank into an easy chair, exuding at every pore an icy and fetid sweat; nausea overpowered him; he could not resist. Summoning his last strength, he dashed out of the parlor, and on the staircase, he relieved himself of the solids and liquids which his employer had gulped down. But in proportion as he emptied his stomach, his monster, like the task-master of the Danaids, continued to fill it. He spread filth and bad odors through the house—in his shame, he dragged himself into the street and gave up his projects of marrying.

Another day the employer was eating almonds and drinking a heavy Spanish wine; Destouches was digesting at the hippodrome of Longchamps, while he watched the horses running; all of a sudden he loses his head, jostles the men, tears the women's dresses and slaps a policeman; he is packed off to the station house to sleep off the wine that his employer had drunk. The next day he is taken before the judge. "If only my drunken master doesn't begin his libations again!" he murmured.

The thing he feared came to pass. The fumes of the wine which ascended from his stomach intoxicated him anew; he insulted the court in full session, he achieved a sentence of two years in prison, for insults to the magistracy, but three days later his all-powerful master secured his release.

The gastric labor of Destouches became every day more difficult and more painful; the ogre repeated his repasts four and five times in the twenty-four hours, and many times a day drank to the point of intoxication. Emile resorted for consolation to the practice of the Romans, he took an emetic, but every time he emptied his stomach, his torturer filled it up again. His life was intolerable. The sight of any food, even bread, gave him nausea.

The disgust which the satiated and impotent feel for the multitude and for everything that lives, cries and moves entered into his soul; he fled from the society of men and the sight of their habitations; he lived alone, in the midst of the fields, going out only at night so as not to meet any living being, man or beast; and night and day he labored to digest the heroic banquets of his employer. The fear of poverty, that faithful companion of his youth, had prevented him from breaking his contract, but he owned himself vanquished, and would gladly have chosen days without bread, rather than this terrible labor, this stomach always digesting. He betook himself to M. Gabarit, determined to break the contract; the notary declared up and down that it was impossible; he was bound for three years more, and even if it killed him, he must go on to the end. By way of consolation he added:

"You complain because you have been reduced to becoming nothing but a digestive apparatus; but all who earn their living by working are lodged at the same sign. They obtain their means of existence only by confining themselves to being nothing but an organ functioning to the profit of another; the mechanic is the arm which forges, taps, hammers, planes, digs, weaves; the singer is the larynx which vocalizes, warbles, spins out notes; the engineer is the brain which calculates, which arranges plans; the prostitute is the sexual organ which gives out venereal pleasure. Do you imagine that the clerks in my office use their intelligence, or that they reflect when they are copying papers ? Oh, but they don't; thinking is not their business; they are nothing but fingers which scribble. They perform in my offices for ten or twelve hours this work which is far from exhilarating, which gives them headaches, stomach disorders and hemorrhoids; and at evening they carry home writing to finish, that they may earn a few cents to pay their landlord. Console yourself, my dear sir, these young people suffer as well as you, and not one of them has the satisfaction of saying that he receives per year the sum that you draw for a single month of digestive labor."

"It is sad, terribly sad, and I have not even the consolation of believing myself the most unhappy of mortals."

"Imprint this truth on your memory; the poor man no longer exists for himself in our civilized societies, but for the capitalist, who sets him to work at his fancy or according to his needs with such or such of his organs." Emile Destouches went out from the office broken-hearted. He wandered through the streets as at that former time when hunger tortured his entrails. Never had he felt so miserable; the present was without joys and the future without hopes. He observed with despair the rapid exhaustion of his vitality, he was emaciated till he had no more than the skin on his bones; the food which he digested did not nourish him, it only traversed his body, leaving behind it a dull sense of hunger, and headaches which made him almost crazy.

While he, with death in his soul, was wandering aimlessly around, his employer, his joyful employer, was eating and drinking, and causing masses of food heavy as lead to fall into his stomach.

"Ah! What miseries! My body racked with pain, disgusted with everything would stop to suffer in peace, but this executioner to whom I have sold more than my soul, imposes upon me labor unceasing. In death alone I shall find repose."

Mad with pain and tired of life, he walked along the wharves; the water attracted him, he threw himself into the river. He was fished out and taken home, calmed by his cold bath.

The next day a solidly built fellow brought him a letter from Sch___ ; it announced to him that from that time to the expiration of his contract of servitude, he would live under the surveillance of the bearer of the letter.

"My little fellow," said his keeper brutally, I am your overseer; no more farces, understand! You no longer belong to yourself, you have sold your appetite and roped in forty-eight thousand plunks, now you have to live and you have no right to kill yourself. If you were to take your life what would become of our employer? The dear man, doesn't he need to digest what he eats? There's no other way. His belly must rest, so yours must work. I give you warning that the first time you try suicide again, I will box you up like a lunatic, those are my orders. But don't worry, you will not grow old at it, I have watched two others before you, and they died at a gallop. What an ogre our capitalist is, by thunder! His appetite comes as he eats, it's all very fine for him; he isn't the one who gets the indigestions. He crams until the digesting machine that he has bought bursts."

'To die of indigestion! That is my future."

A new life began. Like the artisans who work at home for their employer, Emile had up to that time lived with a shadow of liberty, but from that day, like the proletarian imprisoned in his employer's factory, he was to digest under the eye of an overseer. Overwhelmed by the monumental repasts of his employer, he had suspended his hygienic walks, prescribed by the contract; he passed his days and nights, extended at full length, moving only to perform the most necessary physiological functions. But his keeper was commissioned to see to the rigorous execution of the contract that had been drawn up; not a moment of the precious time he had sold was to be wasted. At the break of day he dragged him from his bed and obliged him to take long walks in the fields in order to prepare a morning appetite for the employer. In the afternoon, when filled up to the neck and stretched out on his back, he would have wished to remain motionless, but he was obliged to put himself on the march, in order to promote the current process of digestion and to prepare for his employer a new appetite, fresh and solid. .

Emile had his caprices of revolt.

"Don't kick, my little fellow," said his overseer at the first sign of insubordination, "you are dealing with too strong a party, you will get hurt. I have in my portfolio the doctor's certificates, the orders from police headquarters, the judge's permission, in fact the whole business for chucking you into Charenton! And there I will take you with a club, like the convicts."

Emile, cast down, stupefied, dejected, lived without will power, always digesting, always ill, always trembling, he lay down, rose, walked, stopped, sat at the command of the overseer, submissive and mute like a whipped poodle-dog that dares not bark.

One morning the employer had devoured a breakfast more formidable than usual; he had gobbled down tureenfuls of fish soup and had gorged himself on dishes of cod, kilogrammes of meat and mountains of macaroni. Emile was crushed, he slept heavily for two hours; when his overseer put him on his feet for the regulation walk, this enormous mass of undigested food bore down like a dead weight on his stomach. He went along heavily by the side of his guard, dragging his legs painfully, with his head sadly inclined forward; at a turn of the road he dashed into a group of men and women talking and laughing. Sch___ was strutting along in the center, the gayest of all, his coarse and noisy laugh sounded like a flourish of trumpets, while his fellow revelers were ready to faint from listening.

"What boorish gaiety," said one of them, "would any one believe that this animal has just been murdering himself with victuals that would have been too much for ten peasants who had gone hungry for three days?"

The sight of his employer happy and in good humor inspired Destouches with a resolution, he pressed through the crowd and threw himself at his feet. He wept, related his griefs, his disgust, implored pity, begged that he be delivered from his abominable slavery, offered to return the money that he had received; he asked only one favor, to be allowed to rest, and no longer digest for another.

"What does that lunatic want?" said Sch___ , repulsing him with his foot.

The guard seized Emile by the collar, raised him from the earth and dragged him across several fields. Once at their lodgings, he belabored him with blows.

"That will teach you to trouble the digestion of our employer."
Destouches submitted passively, like a dejected steer; but sometimes even

cattle become enraged.

"I have labored, I have suffered that the other might enjoy, I have endured everything; at the end of my strength I have wept, I have implored, and I have been beaten. Death is near at hand. Come! Take courage, there is nothing to lose."

Escaping from the custody of the overseer, after getting him intoxicated, he runs to the house of his torturer. Sch___ , jocose and rubicund, his body active and his mind cheerful, was about to seat himself at the table. Terror seized him at seeing Emile Destouches, disheveled, haggard, a pistol tightly grasped in his hand.

"Help!—Don't kill me!"

"You coward, you villain, you hog, you glutton! You have tortured me, you have put others to a painful death and you would like to kill more still— you have done your last eating!

With a revolver shot full in his belly, he stretched him on the earth. Thinking him dead, he went to the police office and told his story; the commissioner thought him crazy; his overseer arrived out of breath, and confirmed him in that opinion, which the medical specialists corroborated learnedly. Sch___ , cured of his wound, resumed after a few weeks the course of his exaggerated repasts. Emile Destouches was shut up in Charenton and treated to a course of shower-bath and strait-jacket, for having sold his appetite.

THE END

Cover of the 1913 New York Labor News
edition of *The Religion of Capital*

Simple Socialist Truths
Paul Lafargue

Worker. *But if there were no masters, who would give me work?*

Socialist. That's a question I am often asked; let us examine it. In order to work, three things are required: a workshop, machines, and raw material.

W. *Right.*

S. Who builds the workshop?

W. *Masons.*

S. Who made the machines?

W. *Engineers.*

S. Who grew the cotton you weave, who sheared the wool your wife spins, who dug the mineral your son forges?

W. *Husbandmen, shepherds, miners – workers like myself.*

S. Consequently, you, your wife, and your son can only work because these various other workers have already supplied you with buildings, machinery, and raw material.

W. *That's so; I could not weave calico without cotton and without a loom.*

S. Well then, it is not the capitalist or master who gives you work, but the mason, the engineer, the ploughman. Do you know how your master has procured all that is necessary for your work?

W. *He bought it.*

S. Who gave him the money?

W. *How do I know. His father had left him a little; to-day he is a millionaire.*

S. Has he earned his million by working his machines and weaving his cotton?

W. *Not very likely; it is by making us work that he gained his million.*

S. Then he has grown rich by loafing; that is the only way to make a fortune. Those who work get just enough to live on. But, tell me, if you and your fellow workers did not work, would not your master's machines rust, and his cotton be eaten by insects?

W. *Everything in the workshop would go to wreck and ruin if we did not work.*

S. Consequently, by working you are preserving the machines and raw material necessary for your labour.

W. *That is true; I had never thought of that.*

S. Does your master look after what goes on in his works?

W. *Not much; he makes a daily round to see us at our work, but he keeps his hands in his pockets for fear of dirtying them. In the spinning-mill, where my wife and daughter work, the masters are never seen, although there are four of them; still less so in the foundry, where my son works; the masters are never seen nor ever known; not even their shadow is seen – it is a Limited Liability Company that owns the works. Suppose you and I had five hundred francs saved up, we could buy a share, and become one of the masters, without ever having put, or without putting, a foot in the place.*

S. Who, then, directs and superintends the work in this place belonging to the shareholding masters, and in your own shop of one master, seeing the masters are never there, or so seldom that it doesn't count?

W. *Managers and foremen.*

S. But if it is workers who have built the workshop, made the machines, and produced the raw materials; if it is workers who keep the machines going, and managers and foremen who direct the work – what does the master do, then?

W. *Nothing but twiddle his thumbs.*

S. If there were a railway from here to the moon, we could send the masters there, without a return ticket, and your weaving, your wife's spinning, your son's moulding, would go on as before. Do you know what the profit was realized by your master last year?

W. *We calculate that he must have got a hundred thousand francs.*

S. How many workers does he employ – men, women and children, all included?

W. *A hundred.*

S. What wages do they get?

W. *On an average, about a thousand francs, counting in the salaries of managers and foremen.*

S. So that the hundred workers in the work receive altogether a hundred thousand francs in wages, just enough to keep them from dying of hunger, while your master pocketed a hundred thousand francs for doing nothing. Where did these two hundred thousand francs come from?

W. *Not from the sky; I never saw it rain francs.*

S. It is the workers in his works who have produced the hundred thousand francs they received in wages, and, besides, the hundred thousand francs profit of the master, who has employed part of that in buying new machines.

W. *There is no denying that.*

S. Then it is the workers who produce the money which the master devotes to buying new machines to make them work; it is the managers and foremen, wage slaves like yourself, who direct the production; where, then, does the master come in? What's he good for?

W. *For exploiting labour.*

S. Say rather, for robbing the labourer; that is clearer and more exact.

Cathecism for Investors
That Is to Say, An Instruction, to be Inculcated in the Working People from Early Life.
Paul Lafargue

Question. *What is your name?*

Answer. Wage worker.

Q. *Who are thy parents?*

A. My father was called Wage worker; my mother's name is Poverty.

Q. *Where wast thou born?*

A. In a garret under the roof of a tenement house which my father and his comrades built.

Q. *What is thy religion?*

A. The Religion of CAPITAL.

Q. *What general duties does thy religion enjoin upon thee?*

A. Two principally: first, the duty of Abnegation; second, the duty of Toil. My religion commands me to abdicate my rights to all property on earth, that common mother of us all, to the treasures she bears in her womb, to the product of her surface, to her wonderful fertility through the light and the heat of the sun; it commands me to abdicate my rights of property in the product of the labor of my hands and my brain. My religion commands me to toil from early childhood to my dying day — to toil by sun light, gas light, or electric light, by day and by night; to toil on the earth, under the earth, and in the waters that are under the earth; to toil everywhere and evermore.

Q. Does thy religion lay upon thee any other duties?

A. It lays upon me the further duty of self-denial and privation; to still my hunger only partially; to pinch all my physical wants; and to suppress all my mental aspirations.

Q. Does thy religion forbid thee to taste of certain articles of food?

A. It forbids me to touch game, poultry and meat unless they are of fourth rate quality, and it forbids me to taste at all the better qualities of fish, wine or milk.

Q. What food does it allow thee?

A. Bread, potatoes, beans, herrings, the refuse of the butcher shops and also sausages. To the end that I may stimulate my exhausted strength, it also allows me adulterated wines, beer and similar liquors.

Q. What duties does thy religion lay upon thee with regard to thyself?

A. To retrench my expenses, to live in narrow and spare rooms, to wear torn, tattered and patched up clothes, until they actually fall off my body in shreds. To go about out at toes and heels and without stockings, exposed to the wet and the soilure of the streets and roads.

Q. What duties does thy religion lay upon thee with regard to thy family?

A. To deny my wife and daughters all ornaments of elegance and good taste; to cause them to be dressed in rude materials and with barely enough to escape being hauled up by the police for indecent exposure. To teach them not to shiver in the winter in calicos, and not to smother in the summer in close or topfloor rooms, under tin roofs heated with the heat of the Dog Days. To inculcate in my little ones, from their tenderest years, the sacred principle of toil, to the end that they may be able to earn their living from early childhood, and not become a burden upon society; to teach them to go to bed without a light and supperless; and to accustom them to the misery that is their lot in life.

Q. *What duties does thy religion lay upon thee with regard to society?*

A. To increase the national wealth — first through my toil, and next through my savings as soon as I can make any.

Q. *What does thy religion order thee to do with thy savings?*

A. To entrust them to the savings banks and such other institutions that have been established by philanthropic financiers to the end that they may loan them out to our bosses. We are commanded to place our earnings at all times at the disposal of our masters.

Q. *Does thy religion allow thee to touch thy savings?*

A. As rarely as possible; but it recommends to us not to insist too strongly upon receiving our funds back; we are told we should patiently submit to our fate if the philanthropic financiers are unable to meet our demands, and inform us that our savings have gone up in smoke.

Q. *Who is thy God?*

A. CAPITAL.

Q. *Has He existed since the beginning of time?*

A. Our most learned high priests, the official political economists, say He exists since the creation of the world. At first, however, He was very little, hence His throne was usurped by Jupiter and other Gods. But since about the year 1500, He grew daily into power and glory, and to-day He rules the world according to His will.

Q. *Is thy God omnipotent?*

A. Yes. His grace can grant any and all enjoyments. When He turns His countenance from a person, a family, a country, they are smitten with misery. The power of the God CAPITAL increases with the increase of His bulk. Daily does He conquer new countries; daily does He enlarge the swarms of His vassals, who devote their lives to the mission of increasing His power.

Q. Who are the chosen ones of thy God?

A. The Capitalists — manufacturers, merchants and landlords.

Q. How does thy God reward thee?

A. By furnishing work to me, my wife and my children, down to the youngest.

Q. Is that thy only reward?

A. No. Our God allows us to help still our hunger, by looking through the large pier glass windows of stylish restaurants, devour with our eyes the delightful roasts and delicacies that we have never tasted and never will taste, because these viands are there only for the nourishment of the chosen ones and their high priests. Out of His kindness we are also allowed to warm our limbs, numb with cold, by affording us occasional opportunities to admire the soft fur and the thick-spun woolen cloths exhibited in large stores and intended for the comfort of the chosen ones and their high priests only. He also grants us the exquisite joy of regaling our eyes, on the streets and public resorts, with the sight of the sacred crowds of Capitalists and Landlords, to admire their sleekness and roundness, together with their gorgeously decked lackeys and footmen as they drive by in brilliant equipages.

Q. Are the chosen ones of the same race as thyself?

A. The manufacturers and landlords are kneaded out of the same clay as myself, but they have been chosen out of thousands and millions.

Q. What have they done to deserve this elevation?

A. Nothing. Our God manifests His omnipotence by bestowing His favors upon those who have not earned them.

Q. Then is thy God unjust?

A. CAPITAL is the incarnation of Justice; only, His justice passeth our understanding. CAPITAL is omnipotent. Were He compelled to bestow His grace upon those who earned it, He would be weakened, because then His power would have limits. Consequently, He can show His power in no stronger way than by picking His favorites from among pickpockets and idlers.

Q. *How does thy God punish thee?*

A. By sentencing me to idleness. From that moment I am excommunicated; I then know not where to find food, or where to lay myself down. From that moment I and mine must perish with hunger and want.

Q. *What are the sins that call this punishment upon thy head ?*

A. None. CAPITAL throws me out of work whenever it pleases Him.

Q. *What prayers does thy religion commend to thee?*

A. I pray not with words. My prayer is LABOR. The bare utterance of any other prayer would interfere with my actual prayer — LABOR. This is the only prayer that profits, because it is the only one that pleases CAPITAL and that produces surplus values.

Q. *Where do you pray?*

A. Everywhere. On the fields and in the work-shops; in mills and mines; ashore and at sea. To the end that our prayer be granted, we are in duty bound to lay our freedom, our dignity, our will at the feet of CAPITAL. At the ringing of the bell, at the whistling of the machine, we must hasten to congregate, and, once engaged in prayer, set our arms and legs, hands and feet in motion like automata, we must grunt and swear, we must strain our muscles and exhaust our nerves. At our prayer meetings we must submit with humble mien and patiently to the ill-temper and insults of the boss and his foremen; they are always right. We must never utter a complaint if the boss lowers our wages and raises our hours of work; everything he does is right, and is done for our best. We must consider it an honor if the boss takes undue liberties with our wives and daughters. Rather than ever to allow a complaint to escape our lips, rather than ever to allow our blood to boil, rather than ever to think of striking, we should submit to all trials, swallow our bread moistened with our own spittle only, and drink dirty water to wash that down. Should we be impertinent enough to dare find fault with such treatment, then would our masters scourge us with the prisons and penitentiaries, sharp-cutting sabres, repeating rifles, cannons, policemen's clubs and even the gallows. They would clap us behind the bars if we were to grumble; they would mow us down if we were to do aught that is contrary to the decrees of the laws which they have enacted and promulgated.

Q. Do you expect any reward after death?

A. A very great one. After I am dead CAPITAL allows me to lie down and rest; I am then freed from hunger and cold, and from the fear of want forevermore. I then enjoy the eternal peace of the GRAVE.

Excerpted from Paul Lafargue's *The Religion of Capital* (1887)

A Brief History of Paul Lafargue
Fred Thompson

I. French Labor and Politics, 1830-1880

By 1880 when Lafargue ran as a serial in *L'Egalité* the material that became
the *Right to Be Lazy*, France was a republic run by successful businessmen
and old families. Most of them would have preferred a monarchy on the
English style but they could not agree on either of the two contenders
for the throne. It was the unstable outcome of a century of European
struggles in which those whose hopes lay with the growth of capitalism
had used the working class against their feudal predecessors only to find
that the workers were no longer content with being so used.

The first Napoleon, a few months after the suppression of those who
hoped for workingclass gains in the great revolution, dispersed a royalist
mob with his famous "whiff of grapeshot." He then built an army that
extended his power wherever a business class chafed at old restrictions,
to be defeated by the governments of those countries where the business
class either had won a secure hold or had not yet developed a will to take
control. After Waterloo the European establishment returned the throne
to a Bourbon, Louis XVIII, who was well aware that he must serve the
business class. His brother Charles, who succeeded him in 1824, tried to
restore the older order but the uprising of July 1830 replaced him with
the business king Louis Philippe, who ruled through the machinations of
Guizot and Thiers.

In 1834 when the silk workers of Lyons struck, Thiers as Minister of
Interior and in charge of police spread the false rumor that these workers
had upset the local government. Thus he precipitated a demonstration
by Parisian radicals so that he could mow them down, as depicted by the

artist Daumier in his *Massacre in Rue Trananain*. Any action by workers to
regulate wages had been forbidden in 1793, and Napoleon had reinforced
the ban on union activities in 1810 with severe penalties. These laws
remained, but forbidden union practices and utopian hopes survived.

In February 1848 the business class was unhappy with this regime and the
workers enthusiastically toppled Louis Philippe and Guizot. The action
set off a wave of revolts across Europe. Everywhere it created the same
dilemma: to let the workers do a thorough housecleaning would be to let
workers instead of business rule. One need of the times was to replace a
patchwork of too numerous principalities with nations large enough to
accommodate a growing young capitalism. This led to conflicting national
aspirations that prevented the creation of constitutional national states and
substantially restored the old order. Liberated Hungarians repressed Croats
and Slovaks who then helped Radetzky strangle the progressive movement
in Italy and helped Windesgratz retake Vienna. Ten days after the Emperor's
Slav troops, with the approval of Czech businessmen, had restored order in
Prague, Cavaignac, with the approval of the French business class, started
his massacre of the workers of Paris. Henceforth European business was to
avoid asking labor to help it find a more congenial political environment,
and instead was to select whichever princeling seemed to business most
suitable and make him head of a national federation of lesser states.

The utopian socialism that took the popular fancy in the upsurge of 1848
in Paris was that of Louis Blanc, with its slogan "the Right to Work." He
proposed that the government set up National Workshops for producing
human needs in which that right could be asserted. The plan appealed to
all workers, not only to the large number of unemployed. The new republic
set up these National Workshops but the politicians in charge wanted
neither to assure all a shelter from loss of jobs, nor to compete with their
friends' enterprises in the production of goods. The shops did only work
of little urgency and in effect provided merely charity. When the wave of
revolt through Europe abated they decided to end this so-called socialist
experiment. From June 23 to June 26 troops under General Cavaignac
answered the slogan of "Bread or Lead" with lead. Hundreds were executed

on the Champs de Mars and thousands sent to French penal colonies. The slogan "the Right to Work" persisted; Lafargue's title, The *Right to be Lazy* (la droit à la paresse), was counterposed to it. A century after the June massacre American politicians revived the phrase as their slogan for fighting the union shop.

From the great revolution of 1789 the business class had acquired whatever the church and aristocracy had lost, except for such farmlands as had gone into the family-size holdings on which three-quarters of the population lived as peasants, the most conservative populace in Europe. In the election for president in December 1848 these peasants had their first vote, and the only candidate whose name was known to them was Louis Napoleon, nephew of the military adventurer who had cut three inches off the height of the average Frenchman. Louis Napoleon promised order and was elected. He was an opportunist who had joined the radical Carbonari in Italy, had tried twice previously for the throne of France, had been exiled to England and there volunteered for the special police formed to crush the Chartist demand for votes for workers. Soon the politicians felt urged to restrict the wide franchise. Napoleon saw a third chance at the throne: By promising an impotent universal suffrage on take-it-or-leave-it plebiscites, and by rallying the down-and-outs with beer and sausages into a force to shoot down any workers who resisted him, he managed to talk democracy and yet establish himself as Emperor by a military take-over on December 2, 1851. After his victory 160 resisting workers were executed and 26,000 were transported to penal servitude in the hulks.

In return for serving the business class Napoleon demanded that there be no interference with his dreams of grandeur. During the reign of Louis Philippe extensive canal and railway systems had been laid as foundation for industrial growth, but far more than any other major economy French industry was devoted to the production of luxury goods, a type of industry characterized by long hours, low pay and little mechanization. During the Second Empire (1851-1870) industrial production doubled, but "the average daily wage rose only 30 percent," says Horne in his *Fall of Paris*, "while the cost of living rose a minimum of 45 percent" in Paris. The city was remade with wide avenues that made the barricades of 1830 or 1848 impossible, and with no stones ready to hurl at the forces of repression. Like modern urban renewal plans, these improvements forced workers who had lived in the flea bags that they replaced to hunt up even more cramped and costly flea bags, so that by 1870 rents were reckoned as eating up a third of the typical Paris wage, while food, practically meatless, used up another 60 per cent. The typical workday was eleven hours. A man might earn almost four francs a day, but women only from half a franc to a franc and a quarter, mostly at needlework in hopeless competition with convent labor.

Despite laws forbidding unions (except during a few weeks in 1848), union practices persisted as they had before in such disguises as mutual aid societies or, until the railroads ended the old journeyman tour of France, as the *compagnonnages* that served as secret societies, employment systems, and boarding systems for their members. Until 1874, except in the big industries where it was pointless, there was no law limiting child labor. After 1866 Napoleon faced a series of economic and diplomatic reverses. He began to cater somewhat to labor in hopes of curbing those who threatened his grandiose dreams. With no change in law, local trade groups (syndicats) were allowed to sprout among the more skilled occupations in Paris. By 1870 there were about 70,000 union members in Paris and about as many again in the rest of France. In 1864 in London the first International, the International Working Men's Association, had been founded, with Karl Marx a leading figure, to promote solidarity of workers across frontiers. Many of the French union groups were loosely allied to it, along with some socialist groups not engaged in bargaining about wages. Their typical outlook was a preference for a republic and a Proudhonist hope for freedom from wage servitude by way of self-employment or cooperatives, a change they hoped to achieve without any major social struggle. They made such views dominant in the early congresses of the IWMA. But some of the French IWMA were more militant, such as those who struck in Le Creusot in 1870 at the works of Schneider et Cie, even though that metal works was headed by the president of the Corps Legislatif himself.

In 1870 Napoleon's diplomacy got him into a disastrous war with Prussia. Some of his troops surrendered, and others, instead of remaining mobile with access to food and other supplies, shut themselves up in besieged cities and fortresses. After the surrender at Sedan, September 4, 1870, and the capture of Napoleon, the Legislative Assembly declared the throne vacant. The republican politicians headed for the Hotel de Ville as the traditional spot to declare the republic. There workers raised the red flag, a symbol at that time for democracy from the bottom up. Gambetta, eloquent spokesman for the poor, despite their protests, rallied a sufficient following to replace the red flag with the tricolor of 1792, a clear symbol of what was happening.

A Government of National Defense was formed to resist the Prussian invasion. Its right to office was based on how loud was the vocal acclaim engineered for its candidates from among the happy crowd that surrounded the Hotel de Ville that bright Sunday morning. The workers and radicals wanted to defend the city. Throughout the country the gentry felt that since they could not hope to win the war it would be best to settle it before it ate up more of their assets. The cotton masters of Rouen and Lille, according to Lafargue, were happy to see the more efficient cotton industry of Alsace, with a third of the nation's spindles, surrendered to the enemy and thus kept outside the tariff wall they promptly erected.

Paris was besieged, its population immediately swollen by a half. Gambetta ballooned out to build up the needed resistance of a mobile military force in the provinces. In this city surrounded by Prussian troops those with money ate delicacies and those without money ate rats. But housewives donated their kettles to be made into cannon for the defense of Paris, and Victor Hugo started a popular subscription to procure the manufacture of two hundred cannon for the National Guard. It was an armed population that felt it owned its arms. Balloons were sent up, designed to fall into Prussian hands, with these messages in German: "Crazy people, shall we always throttle each other for the pleasure and pride of kings?" and "Paris defies her enemy; all France is rising; death to invaders."

An armistice January 27 brought in food for those who had money, but most Parisians had neither money nor work. Yet Favre had to tell Bismarck that it would mean civil war if he tried to disarm the National Guard. Bismarck advised, "Provoke an uprising then while you have an army with which to repress it." The new National Assembly elected to make peace with the victor was largely royalist or Bonapartist. It took no action to ease the insufferable situation of the workers. Instead it enacted a Law of Maturities ending a wartime moratorium on debts, making them now payable on demand and letting landlords demand payment of all accumulated rent. This put a host of "white collar" workers into the same situation as the manual workers.

On February 26 Thiers signed the peace treaty. As he did so an apprehensive National Guard, singing the *Marseillaise*, seized the two hundred cannon that belonged to them and hauled them to the workingclass *arondissement* of Montmartre for safekeeping. They were concerned especially because the peace terms provided for a humiliating victory march of German troops through their city. (During the siege, on January 18, Germany as a nation had been born.) On March 8 Thiers ordered the regular army to remove those guns. The adjourned Assembly had moved to Versailles but most government offices remained in Paris. On March 17 Thiers assigned 18,000 troops, most to cover likely foci of an uprising, and one body to steal into Montmartre at four in the morning to seize those cannon. They did so, but had no horses to haul them away. Louise Michel grasped this breathing space to spread the alarm, with the result that the populace protested and the troops fraternized.

One of the popular National Guard had been wounded, and Clemenceau, the local mayor, wanted to take him away for first aid. General Lecomte, in charge of the attempted seizure, refused the mayor's request and the populace dragged him from his horse and executed him. With Lecomte was Clement Thomas, who had been hated for twenty-three years for his role in the slaughter of workers in 1848, and he too was killed. This was the only blood shed in the revolt of Paris until the fighting of the last few days of May.

Thus a new administration of the city was born. It adopted the name of the administration of the city in 1792 – the Commune of Paris. Commune is an old French term meaning a self-governing community; it had nothing to do with communism. It invited the rest of France to create similar bases for a federation. It sought autonomy enough for Paris to assure that a conservative countryside could not deprive it of freedom of speech and assembly. On behalf of it Clemenceau and the mayors of other *arondissements* tried to negotiate with Thiers, but he offered no concessions. Instead, Thiers bombarded his own capital and in the last week of May sent in his troops to massacre its citizens. In this he had the backing of Bismarck, who let Thiers increase his army to double that allowed by the terms of armistice, then released 400,000 prisoners of war, from whom Thiers could readily recruit men to do his bidding. Bismarck stationed Prussian troops to the Commune's rear, first to cut off food, and in the days of the final massacre to cut off escape.

The main concerns of the Commune had to be military, but it put Elisée Reclus, the anarchist geographer, in charge of libraries, and Courbet, the realist painter, in charge of art – he arranged the pulling down of that Bonapartist symbol, the Vendôme Column, and so had to spend the rest of his life outside France. Leo Frankel was put in charge of reopening the workshops as cooperatives, and he abolished night work for bakers. Vaillant made unused plans for free education. Jourde and Varlin kept scrupulous accounts for the Commune, and borrowed enough money from the Bank of France to keep the Commune running; the Bank preferred this to seizure. Few of the Commune members were with the IWMA and fewer of these were Marxist. Their inspiration came from the jailed Blanqui, the dead Proudhon, the repeated experience – 1789, 1830 and 1848 – of the fruits of their blood-won victories being stolen from them by the very rich, or from the situation at hand, and the desire for a city in which men might speak their thoughts freely.

In taking Paris from its citizens, Thiers' forces killed between twenty and twenty-five thousand. They made an additional forty thousand march without food or water, many of them wounded, and many dying on the way, to Camp Satory. There Gallifet picked out those he chose for immediate slaughter for the edification of the elegant ladies from Versailles, who came there to watch. After a grim winter in the hulks, half of the forty thousand were acquitted. The last execution of prisoners was in 1874 and the last trial in 1875; 2,510 drew forced labor for life; 1,160 drew imprisonment in fortified places, involving latrine duty in garrisons; 3,417 were sent to overseas penal colonies, mostly in New Caledonia; about 5,000 more drew lesser sentences. Somehow the European press managed to describe this as the brutality of the Communards, not the sadism of the French upper classes; British descriptions of the Commune led the British unions to withdraw from the IWMA, assuring its decline.

To this day pilgrimages are made each May 28 to the Mur des Federes at Père Lachaise cemetery, where the last defenders of the Commune were slaughtered. It is the custom to sing the *Internationale*, written by Eugene Pottier in one inspired sitting in a shack on the outskirts of Paris as the final shots were being fired. As a lad of fourteen he had fought in the July uprising of 1830, and again in the February revolt of 1848; he had defended Paris against Bismarck, and again against the combination of Bismarck and Thiers, and each time he had seen workers die and bankers take the plums. Another workman, Degeyter, set it to the tune now known around the globe.

Repression reigned. No unions met. The IWMA was banned and Thiers tried to have it outlawed worldwide. But the massacre had so cut down the supply of skilled workers that they held a good bargaining position, much as the Black Death of the fourteenth century created what E. Thorold Rogers called the golden age of English labor. Local syndicates of a non-political, non-ideological sort arose, asserting an *ouvrierisme* akin to much American blue-collar thinking today. When amnesty in July 1880 let political refugees return, unions continued zealously to guard their independence from politically-minded intellectuals. This sense of union self-reliance, impregnated with the anarchist ideas of such men as Pelloutier and Griffuelhues, and the somewhat Gallicized Marxism of Lafargue, was to create the distinctive French syndicalist movement of the years preceding World War I. But as of 1880, when *The Right to be Lazy* was written, the minds of most French workers were taken up with their daily routines, bitter memories, a general distrust of Germans, and some hopes for what was called the "English week," with Saturday afternoons off.

II. About Paul Lafargue

In October 1865 the first International Congress of Students was held at Liège. Among those present was Paul Lafargue, who had come to the Congress with some of his republican minded fellow students. All were suspended for their individual and collective insults to church and government, Paul for two years.

At Liège he met a fellow student, Charles Longuet, who was later to become his brother-in-law, and who at the time was an able spokesman for the views of Proudhon. Proudhon had just ended a quarter-century agitation for a decentralized, mutualist, federal, stateless, cooperative economy, and his hope of achieving it without major social struggles was the most popular of the current radicalisms in France. At Liege Paul also met Auguste Blanqui, who had spent much of his sixty years in jail as spokesman for an alternative view: conspiratorial seizure of power. Paul was soon deep in the work in France of the International Working Men's Association. Since its founding in London in September 1864 its center of communication remained there. When Paul went to England in February 1866 to complete the studies in medicine from which he was now banned in France, he became an active IWMA officer. On March 6 he was elected to its General Council, and on March 26, because of his fluency in the Spanish of his boyhood, he was made IWMA secretary for Spain.

Paul had been born January 15, 1842 in Santiago de Cuba. He was proud of a mixed ancestry. His father, a conservative Bordeaux landowner, was the son of a mulatto mother who had fled to New Orleans from what is now Haiti when her husband, a French planter, was killed there. Paul's mother, Virginia, was the daughter of a Carib mother and Abraham Armagnac, a "blue-eyed, fair-haired" French Jew, born in what was then Santo Domingo. Paul's lineage showed in his husky frame, dusky skin and prominent eyes. His ideas he got from his times.

In England he and others who had fled the repressive regime of Louis Napoleon made up their own London French Section of the International, and as Proudhonists quarreled with Marx and the General Council. In 1847, besides producing the *Communist Manifesto,* Marx had published a bitter criticism of Proudhon's *Philosophy of Poverty* under the title *Poverty of Philosophy,* and the bitterness had continued to Proudhon's death in 1865. The French Section in London rebuked the General Council for supporting Polish nationalism when Poland still retained serfdom after Russia had ended it; they said that nationalism was now an obsolete idea and that we should aim at the individualization of humanity. Marx ridiculed what he called "the Proudhonized Stirnerism" of Longuet and Lafargue, but his friend Engels and Marx's daughters welcomed the expatriates more warmly. In August Paul and Laura Marx announced their engagement. It was agreed that Paul should finish his medical studies before they married, but they did so a bit ahead of schedule, with Engels as witness, on April 2, 1868. (Longuet married Jennie, eldest of the three daughters, in 1872, and Edward Aveling, translator of much of Marx's and Engels's writings, later married the third daughter, Eleanor.)

Paul took his finals July 22, 1868 and for a while practiced medicine in London. He went to France hoping to get his degree also at Strasbourg, was in Paris when the Franco-Prussian war broke out, and at his family residence in Bordeaux when the Empire fell. With its fall Longuet returned to become an officer in the National Guard and defend Paris first against the Prussians and then against Thiers. Soon after the Commune was declared Paul went to Paris, but was urged to return to keep up a campaign on behalf of the Commune in the provinces, an effort he had already made through *La Tribune de Bordeaux.* After the fall of the Commune he made his way to the border and was smuggled into Spain by muleteers.

In Spain, on August 11, 1871 he was arrested at Huesca and held for ten days. Had he not been released, he later wrote Engels, a secret society there was ready to paralyze the police and set him free. He busied himself in Spain, largely at Engels's direction, combating Bakunin's anarchist influence in the IWMA, for the Marxists and Bakuninists were struggling for control. On March 11, 1872 Engels wrote Laura Lafargue: "Paul's presence in Madrid at the decisive moment was of incalculable value. . . Had Bakunin carried the day in Spain – and without Paul that was likely – then the split would have been complete."

Lafargue's correspondence with Engels in this period has many references to how police spies had penetrated Bakuninist organizations. He mentioned this infiltration frequently in later years even after Pelloutier had given French anarchism a workingclass outlook and taken it away from the bankrobbers. He fought the anarchists at the Hague Congress of the IWMA, 1872, which he attended with credentials from Spain. Franz Mehring, a close friend of the Lafargues in their later days, calls the report that Lafargue and Engels prepared on the relation between these two factions for the 1873 Geneva convention a compilation of anti-Bakunin rumor and gossip in which no Marxist should take pride.

Paul's Proudhonist background, his libertarian bent, his animal spirits and spontaneity, made him in many ways akin to Bakunin. In 1883 Marx referred jokingly to his two sons-in-law, Paul as the last Bakuninist and Longuet as the last Proudhonist. The Lafargues were close friends of the daring anarchist Louise Michel, and on one occasion Paul was a fellow defendant with her. Despite Lafargue's war with anarchism, it is not surprising that the last movement printing of this pamphlet in America was by Chicago's Solidarity Bookshop (1969), and that this pamphlet has in recent European printings been considered a forerunner of the attitudes of the New Left, of Herbert Marcuse, and others who recognize that revolutionists today reject the culture alike of Puritanism and Madison Avenue as well as the economics of Wall Street and the politics of the Pentagon. In 1882 Paul wrote Engels about his anarchist associates in Paris: "Many think like us but it is a feather they like to wear in their hats." In April 1911 he was urging that Gustave Hervé, noted then as an anti-militarist anarchist, be given an editorial position on *Humanité*. Marxist he became, and his reputation is mainly that of a popularizer of

Marxism; party builder he became, too – and insistent that the party serve immediate and long-run needs of the workers, and never the convenience of bourgeois politicians who might like to borrow its support and yet a champion of socialist unity. But beyond all these Lafargue aimed to build a movement in which there was scope for those of his fellow rebels with whom he disagreed.

After the 1872 Congress Lafargue returned to London. He had given up the practice of medicine. Mehring attributed this to the loss of both the children born to him and Laura. With Laura he tried to make a living from a photo engraving and lithographic shop. But through the years in London and the years in Paris life was hard, and he repeatedly had to ask Engels for money to pay his rent and buy their food. He remained in England even after the July 1880 amnesty, but during these years was actively seeking a hearing for Marxist ideas in France and among French *emigres*. The groundless accusation in the press that Marx in London had been arranging and steering the 1871 revolt in Paris at last was making Marx somewhat known in France. The *Communist Manifesto* had appeared in French in 1847 but went unheeded, with no new French edition until 1882. Marx's 1847 critique of Proudhon had appeared only in French and was written for a French audience, but had received little attention. Guesde, slowly turning from Blanquism toward Marxism, launched a socialist weekly, *L'Egalité*, in 1877, but it ran only thirty-one issues. When he revived it for another thirty-two issues in 1880 Lafargue from London contributed the material for this pamphlet. In this same English period Lafargue's enthusiasm for a portion of Engels's 1877 dispute with Duhring led to the separate publication of this material in *La Revue Socialiste* as *Socialism: Utopian and Scientific*. Since then in many languages this selection has proved the favorite statement of Marxist thought on the ways of history and their relation to the socialist hope.

In 1882 the Lafargues returned to Paris where Paul for a few months had a job with an insurance company writing stilted correspondence much to his distaste. A merger ended that, but during the summer it had enabled him to serve on three socialist publications without pay. He was also trying to earn something with writings on less controversial subjects. He had started his studies on American agriculture and was soon considered something of an expert on that.

Marx visited both sons-in-law in France that summer. Longuet had a job on Clemenceau's *Justice*. Paul's prime concern was, with his convert Guesde, to build a party and paper to promote the Marxist view of a working class becoming aware that they had an historic mission to end capitalism. He and Guesde with that hope went in October 1882 to the St. Etienne Congress of their Parti Ouvrier Francais. There they lost out to those who would submerge their revolutionary hope in the sort of demands it would be possible to achieve at once. This circumstance led to the winners there being called *Possibilistes* and the Marxist losers being called *Impossibilistes*. These *Impossibilistes* immediately held a congress in Rouen to build the sort of party they wanted.

Guesde and Lafargue had lectured at public meetings during both these congresses, and for this the two, along with Dormoy, a republican recently converted to their cause, were charged on the basis of their advocacy of social seizure of the industries with incitement to pillage. For several weeks Paul knew the police were planning to arrest the two of them, but kept on with his activities. On December 12, as he was bringing home food for lunch, he was arrested.

The trial started April 27, 1883. Paul's letters showed that he enjoyed it. The town theater was given free to the defendants for a public meeting on the eve of the trial. There Paul's lecture on how the productivity of American farmers menaced French agriculture was well received. The trial required three sessions, one of them at night, "and coming away from the hearing at 10:30," he wrote Engels, "we were escorted to the hotel by a large and very sympathetic crowd." There was much laughter in the court when the prosecutor read passages from Lafargue's 1872 squib, *Pope Pius IX in Paradise*. But they were found guilty and each of the three given a six-month sentence, with Paul in addition to pay a fine of one hundred francs.

They had until May 21 to serve sentence. Sainte-Pélagie had miserable quarters for debtors and ordinary prisoners, and a smaller part that had been used for years for dissident journalists and other politicals. They went ahead of time to inspect the place and found the jailer to be an admirer of Guesde from his 1878 stay there with Deville for attending the international congress. They reserved the two best rooms in the politicals' section and Lafargue wrote Engels: "They are quite spacious and lit by two fine windows, but they are bare. We shall be allowed to bring in furniture. I shall take my desk and the armchair Mrs Engels gave me. We shall be allowed visitors from 10 to 4 each day." During their six-months' stay they received hampers of wine and delicacies from admirers and, except when she went to London, Laura brought them their lunch each day. It was probably their most carefree time. Civilization today should treat its dissidents at least as well.

Under these not too unhappy circumstances Lafargue rewrote *The Right to be Lazy*, and this may explain the light tone in which it makes its very serious contention. Some may note that quite a number of those lampooned in the text had died between the 1880 and 1883 editions; Girault's 1970 Paris edition annotates the differences between the two. Lafargue did much reading during this prison stay that would show up in his varied writings of later years, and also during his return to Sainte-Pélagie for another four months in summer of 1885, without companions, because he had not paid the hundred-franc fine. On this occasion he feared he might be classed as a debtor, not as a political, and so not admitted to this "Pavilion des Princes," but he was back in his old quarters.

During the 1885 imprisonment, Victor Hugo died. While the nation was pantheonizing the poet, Lafargue wrote an attack on him for a labor paper, and elaborated it into another jail-written pamphlet, *The Legend of Victor Hugo*. Hugo was humanist, liberal, popular; he had urged amnesty for the Communards; his pen had helped destroy the Second Empire; he had initiated the popular subscriptions by which the cannon seized March 18, 1871 were the property of the National Guard, thus unwittingly triggering the Commune – and he had then gone to Belgium disowning both Paris and Versailles. Lafargue's attack expressed the general socialist attitude of the times. Two weeks earlier four demonstrators had been killed by the police and many wounded, all on the grounds that the police thought they might unfurl hidden red flags in their annual procession to the Wall of the Federals to commemorate the 1871 massacre of their comrades. Regarding the Hugo veneration, Laura wrote: "All the socialist and revolutionary organizations decided to take no part in the funeral procession of this greatest of all charlatans, this reactionary humbug." In these mid-1880's Lafargue widened the audience for Marxist socialism. His Paris lectures were reported in the *New York Volkzeitung*. In Bax's British journal *Today* he answered Herbert Spencer's warning that socialism was the "Coming Slavery." Molinari, editor of the *Journal des Economistes* was so orthodox that during the siege of Paris he met Blanquist agitation for food rationing with the argument that "rationing by dearness" was the effective way to handle food shortages, yet in July 1884 he published Lafargue's researches on American wheat production. When Leroy-Beaulieu came out that year with a book against Marx, Molinari let Lafargue answer with twelve pages in the September issue. Engels urged Lafargue to avoid any invective that might provide grounds for refusing publication, but Lafargue wanted to "hold up to ridicule the official economics and its most reputable spokesmen." He wrote that "Laura was astonished that my article with its insults and its frivolous tone was accepted and published without change." In the same scholarly journal he was to reply later to Maurice Block's attack on Marxism. In preparing these answers he had the assistance of Engels, who was at the time hard at work on Marx's unpublished manuscripts for the unfinished portions of *Capital*. Engels wrote Laura: "Paul's reply to Block is excellent, not only in style but in subject matter. People have different ways of learning things, and if he learns political economy by lighting, it's all right so that he does learn it." In all that Paul wrote a light touch of irreverence won him ears that otherwise would have been closed to him. Between jail terms in 1884 he issued his *Course in Social Economy*.

On April 4, 1886 two newspaper reporters investigating a strike at Decazeville, then somewhat over a month old, were charged with having "supported. . . a preconcerted cessation of work with the purpose of forcing an increase in wages or impairing the free function of industry and labor." It was a strike, as Laura wrote to Engels, that was "doing wonders in the way of healing differences between the various groups and sections." On April 17 each of the reporters was sentenced to fifteen months imprisonment. On May 2 a socialist electoral congress drew lots to determine which of the two to pick for their candidate for deputy; with 100,795 votes the chosen journalist almost won the election. During this agitation Lafargue and Guesde were once charged with "inciting to pillage" along with Susini and Louise Michel. Only Louise appeared for trial, but all four were sentenced. The other three appealed and thus appeared before the Assize Court September 24, 1886. All made speeches about the dynamics of history and the economics of capitalism to distinguish between the incitement to pillage, with which they were charged, and the socialist proposal that the workers take possession of the industries they had built and use them for the common good. All three were acquitted.

In elections at that period a jail record helped a workingclass candidate, especially uniting support from the left. The old and often jailed Blanqui had paved the way for the 1880 amnesty by winning his post as deputy for Bordeaux running from jail in 1879. Dormoy, who had been jailed with Guesde and Lafargue, became town councillor in 1888 and later Mayor of Montlucon. At Calais Delecluze was elected to the town council from jail, imprisoned for his action in the strike of the net-makers. And Lafargue's own electoral success was to be sent to the Chamber of Deputies from a prison cell in 1891. Meanwhile he faced the routine campaign defeats, in 1885 running as deputy from Allier, in 1887 as a municipal candidate in Paris, in 1889 as deputy from Armand. He was able to run from Armand only on the promise to repay campaign expenses to local backers from his salary as deputy if elected; in those days campaign expenses were less than the salary of the post sought.

Lafargue and his fellow Guesdists had a paper only off and on. They did not follow the winds of popular concern. These were tense political times, with widespread fear that a dictatorship might be established by

Boulanger, whose public image was inseparable from the magnificent horse that he rode. He drew substantial workingclass support from his efforts to improve the conditions of conscripted sons and brothers, and from his chauvinist talk of taking back both Alsace and Lorraine. A united front urged that no labor candidates compete so that Ferry could defeat Boulanger. Lafargue's articles (May 1888) argued that the conditions necessary for a return of Bonapartism were not present, and the Guesdists, on the slogan "Neither Ferry nor Boulanger," issued leaflets where they ran no candidate and instead urged a vote for Boulanger's horse. This attitude, out of step with the times, worried Engels. Later Lafargue was to take a similar view of the Dreyfus case – that it was an upper-class squabble of little concern to labor. In 1889 he was to follow this outlook through to success in his arrangements for the congress to found the Second International.

In 1887 the German Social-Democrats had proposed a world congress of socialists in the following year; Lafargue convinced Liebknecht to postpone it until July 14, 1889, the centenary of the Fall of the Bastille, and to hold it in Paris during the Paris Exhibition. The Possibilists planned a congress at the same time for the unions; Liebknecht was anxious to attend this and so urged the Guesdists to merge theirs with it. But the Guesdists wanted the Congress to establish that world socialism was now a Marxist movement, aiming by class struggle to achieve revolutionary social change, while Lafargue described the Possibilists (who had been granted city funds to hold their congress) as "carpetbaggers who use socialism to obtain political positions and municipal grants." Liebknecht feared that the Possibilist congress would be much larger, and that a clash might develop between two bodies with patriot French union members attacking the German delegates at the other congress for being German. Again Engels was worried at Lafargue's intransigence but happy with the outcome, for the Guesdist-sponsored congress was the larger, and it set up the Second International. It was attended (by mistake, according to Samuel Gompers, the conservative US labor leader) by Gompers' envoy, who urged the congress to arrange for worldwide demonstrations on May First for the eight-hour day. This proposal was adopted and remains one enduring outcome.

The fight for the shorter workday had to be international as the employers in each country insisted they could not grant the eight-hour day because of foreign competition. It created a natural opportunity for Marxians to spread their ideas about the length of the work day and its relation to the production of surplus value, or the irrepressible conflict of class interests associated with this, the working class as a worldwide class with a global destiny and its victory indispensable to the survival of human values. May Day 1890 was observed in all European countries as the first world labor day, with fear expressed in almost every major newspaper, but with little violence, and that not on the part of the workers. In England the observation was on Sunday, May 4; many unions joined, and Lafargue addressed the great London demonstration to prolonged and vigorous applause.

The next year in April the Guesdists held meetings where they could to make arrangements for large May Day demonstrations again. For this purpose Lafargue went to the textile town of Fourmies, where the workday ran to eleven hours, and held advance meetings. The May Day demonstrations were peaceful all over France, except for Fourmies. There the militia fired on the demonstrators, killing ten, one of these a child of twelve, and wounding thirty-six. More workers would have been killed, but one of the two detachments refused to obey the order to shoot, and most of the other fired over the heads of the crowd, so that most of those killed and wounded must have been shot by officers. One private, a native of Fourmies, explained that he had not shot "because his mother might be in the crowd."

None of those responsible for killing these workers were brought to trial. Lafargue and Culine, the local organizer of the Parti Ouvrier, were charged with incitement to riot in their speech arranging for the demonstration. The chief allegation was that Lafargue had advised any young man called into the army and ordered to shoot at workers to turn around and shoot the other way. Lafargue had made no such statement, but another speaker, Menard, thinking he may have said something of the sort, wrote Lafargue a letter saying so, and that the prosecution had arrested the wrong man.

Lafargue refused to use the letter, and on July 30, 1891 he went once more to Sainte-Pelagie Prison under a one-year sentence and a 1200-franc fine.

On October 20, with the support of all the various radicals, he was elected to the Chamber of Deputies, and released from jail. He participated in forming a coalition of anti-establishment deputies of various parties to fight the routine blocking of all measures that they introduced. In general his behavior was unparliamentary, and not considered effective, and he was not re-elected. The salary did for two years attend to his and Laura's needs. His medical interests showed up in unsuccessful efforts to set up something similar to the London Board of Health.

In 1892 Lafargue published *Communism and the Economic Revolution*, and in 1895 an extensive debate with Jean Jaurès on idealism and materialism in the processes of history. He declined nomination in 1896; in 1898 he did not get enough votes to qualify as a candidate, and that year, with nationalism still in its ascendancy, neither Jaures nor Guesde were elected. In 1899, however, the lies against Dreyfus had been exposed and Waldeck-Rousseau organized his "Cabinet of Republican Defense," inviting the socialist Millerand to be a member of the Cabinet. This precipitated a crisis in the socialist movement. Could socialists accept as ministers to carry out the policies of a non-socialist parliament? The question was aggravated in this instance by the presence of General Gallifet, butcher of the Communards, on this "Cabinet of Republican Defense." In his 1899 book, *The Conquest of Public Power*, Lafargue answered with a strong *no*. Later his position was confirmed by the Socialist International at its 1904 congress in Amsterdam, and this in turn led to the unification of the socialist movement in France, when Jaures' acceptance of this decision made this possible the following year. In 1906 Lafargue ran against Millerand for deputy; Millerand won, two to one. Lafargue's concern for the abatement of inter-socialist friction expressed itself in an essay he published in 1904 in Kautsky's *Neue Zeit* as *The Historical Materialism of Karl Marx*, an undogmatic exposition of economic determinism as a tool for research and definitely not a set of theorems. It was published in France in 1907 as *The Historical Method of Marx* and, in the U.S., in the

International Socialist Review (published by Charles H. Kerr), in fall of the
same year.

After 1895 life became easier for the Lafargues. Engels left Laura a bequest
with which she bought a home in a workingclass suburb; Paul received a
small inheritance and began to get something from his writings. Most of
his writing continued to be his unpaid contributions to the socialist press.
After the 1905 unity of the principal socialist factions in France, most of
these went to Jaurès' *Humanité* and seldom to Guesde's papers. There was
no separation in principle between the two old jailbirds; it was socialist
unity that pulled them apart, issues of Marxist strategy within a synthetic
party that ultimately led to a sharp break a fortnight before Paul's suicide.
He was close to seventy and found the infirmities of old age painful, and
doubted whether he would be of much more use to the movement. He
told Laura of his intentions and she did not want to remain after him.
They wrote warm notes to some close comrades and ended their lives with
a hypodermic of cyanide of potassium. Their funeral brought a mass of
comrades together. One of the less known, of a score of orators there, was
a Russian emigré who had visited them at their home, Vladimir Lenin.

Glossary

Notes on Persons and Places
Compiled by Fred Thompson

Blanqui, Jérome Adolphe (1798-1854). Economist; inherited the academic chair of I. B. Say; made extensive investigations of workingclass conditions and, though ordinarily opposed to government intervention, felt it necessary to protect workers. Referred to by Lafargue as academician to avoid confusion with his brother, the well known Louis

Auguste Blanqui (1805-1881), outstanding revolutionist jailed a large part of his life, including the entire period of the Commune, and then for eight years more.

Borinage, the west half of the Belgian province of Hainaut; like the Charleroi basin, east half of same region, a mining, steel and textile area. See further note under Charleroi.

Boucicaut, Mme. Widow of the merchant (1810-1877) who founded the Bon Marche, the celebrated emporium. She continued it up to 1887 and left a large fortune to its employees.

Broglie, Albert duc de (1821-1901). Supporter of Orleanist claim to the throne; premier 1873-74 and 1877, during persecution of the Communards.

Cassagnac, Paul Grenier de (1843-1904). Bonapartist journalist, like his father a notorious bully and duelist among his victims was the republican leader Flourens who, however, survived. After 1871 he edited *Le Pays* until it was stopped in 1874 for the violence of its articles; in 1876 he supported McMahon's plot to overthrow the Republic.

Chagot, Louis Jules (1801-1877) ran metal-working establishments at Creusot before 1836 when Schneider's enterprises were established there; represented Saone-et-Loire in Bonaparte regime.

Charleroi (see also Borinage). Battleground four times: Revoluionary army took it from Germans June 25, 1794; on June 15, 1815 the French took it on eve of Waterloo; taken by Germans August 22, 1914, but mentioned here because in 1867 "the mineowners of the Charleroi Basin goaded their miserably paid workers into revolt and then let loose the armed forces against them"; the IWMA gave what support it could in "the panic-stricken reign of terror which followed" (Mehring, *Karl Marx*, 393). Lafargue's reference to barracks location corresponds to similar development of the barracks system in England in 1819, when soldiers refused to shoot down neighbor-women during bread riots, the Hessian troops were brought in to flog the British soldiers; they performed the same service in the U.S. following the railroad strikes of 1877.

Cherbuliez, A. E. (1797-1869). Economist and author of several optimistic pamphlets, in the style of Bastiat, attacking socialism, Clemenceau, Georges (1841-1929). "The tiger" of 1919 was mayor of Montmartre when the Communards seized their guns in March 1871; he tried to negotiate between the Commune and Thiers; a radical republican who employed Lafargue's brother-in-law, Longuet, on his newspaper in 1880.

Comte, Auguste (1798-1857). Philosopher; originally a disciple of utopian socialist Saint-Simon; later founded the influential school called Positivism. His classification of knowledge provided the basis for the synthetic philosophy of Herbert Spencer and Lester Ward. Comte's followers in the 1870's were occupied with preaching patience and optimism to the oppressed.

Dolfuss. A leading family in the industrial city of Mulhouse (q.v.) and its chemical industry. Its members served as mayor on several occasions; Jean Dolfuss wrote on economics.

Dufaure, Jules A. S. (1798-1881). A supporter of Thiers; Minister of Public Works in 1839, promoted rail construction; supported the Republic in 1848; member of National Assembly in 1871; Minister of "Justice" under Thiers, and Premier in 1876. In 1879 he forced the resignation of Pres. McMahon for plotting against the Republic. Dufaure's cabinet fell in 1876 as a result of Gambetta's income-tax proposal, and the demand for freedom of conscience and worship as well as amnesty for the Communards.

Ferry, Jules (1832-1893). Republican politician and promoter of colonial expansion; as Minister of Education (1879-80) founded the secular school system; was premier for two periods in the 1880's; was part of the government of September 4, 1870, and had to steal away from the Hotel de Ville in March 1871 after Thiers left for Versailles. Marx in his Civil War in France (Kerr edition, 56) says: "Jules Ferry, a penniless barrister before the 4th of September, contrived as mayor of Paris, during the siege, to job a fortune out of famine."

Freycinet, Charles (1828-1923). Mining engineer; wrote on child and female labor in England; supporter of Gambetta; Minister of Public Works under Dufaure; promoted three-milliard scheme for government acquisition of existing railroads and construction of new ones.

Gallifet, Gaston Alexandre Auguste, Marquis de, Prince des Martignes (1830-1909). Notorious as the butcher of the Communards; served Napoleon III in Mexico, Italy and Algeria; in 1872 suppressed an Algerian rebellion; later a favorite crony of Edward VII.

Gambetta, Leon (1838-1882). Rose to prominence in 1868 when he defended Delescluze, who had opened a fund in his paper to provide a tombstone for Baudin, who had been shot on the barricades in 1851. Gambetta's defense of Delescluze ridiculed the government and, being timed with the economic and political reverses of the government, turned the tide against Napoleon III. In September 1870 he made himself Minister of the Interior (in charge of police), and in October took over the Ministry of War, ballooned out of Paris to direct resistance to the Prussians; he did not support Thiers or Versailles. A consistent republican, in September 1870 he took down the red flag when it was raised and replaced it with the tricolor of revolutionary France of 1792. He urged amnesty for the Communards, introduced the bill in 1880 that granted it, and before that promoted funds for their relief in exile. At 1879 Congress of Berlin he championed Greece against the Ottoman Empire, and was thus suspected by Lafargue of aiding reactionary Russia.

Germiny, Charles-Gabriel Lebeque, Comte de (1789-1871). Minister of Finance many times, including 1840, during the brief Republic of 1848, and under Napoleon III. Reference could be to his son, who in 1877 skipped to Brazil after conviction.

Girardin, Emile de (1806-1881). Promoter of low-priced journals, usually following trends of public opinion, but in 1851 he did pioneer the idea of a general strike in France; later supported by Napoleon III. In the 1870's his mass journals were usually pro-Republic.

Guesde, Jules (1845-1922). A journalist who founded in 1877 the socialist weekly journal *L'Egalité*. In 1880 he joined Paul Lafargue to establish the Workers Party and in 1893 he was elected to the Chamber of Deputies.

Guizot, Francois (1787-1874) ran cabinet 1840-48; the reference presumably is to his recurrent advice: enrichez-vous (work, make money, and if you don't have a vote now, you will if you get rich). Under Louis Philippe he thwarted all democratic trends, and was dumped in the revolt of 1848.

Hugo, Victor (1802-1885). Best known in the U.S. for his 1862 novel *Les Miserables* that depicts at one point the 1830 July uprising; best known in France as poet and liberal agitator. In exile during Second Empire he coined the title, "Napoleon the Little," and returned as a hero to France after downfall of the Empire.

He launched the fund for the National Guard to buy their own cannon which was the basis for their refusal to surrender them during the Paris Commune. As a member of the Versailles Assembly he refused to ratify the treaty with Prussia, and withdrew from the Assembly March 8 when it refused to seat Garibaldi. During Commune he retreated to Brussels unallied either with revolutionary Paris or Versailles. After fall of the Commune he urged amnesty; wrote a major poem on 1871, *L'Année Terrible*. On Hugo's death Lafargue wrote from prison a pamphlet, *The Legend of Victor Hugo*, assailing him as a fraud. This pamphlet later appeared in German translation (Neue Zeit, April-June 1888).

Jujurieux. Town in Department of the Ain; chief industry: casting off of silk.

Kestner, G. M. J. S. (1803-1870). Paternalistic owner of chemical industry founded by his father at Thann; elected to represent Haut-Rhein.

Kock, Paul de (1793-1871). Novelist and author of melodramas, noted for his depictions of bourgeois life.

Koechlin, Eugene (1815-1885). Like Dolfuss, head of a leading capitalist family at Mulhouse; ran Koechlin Frères (brothers); mayor in 1870; represented Mulhouse at the Bordeaux Assembly.

Langlois, Amedée, Jerome (1819- ?). Collaborated with Proudhon on the latter's paper, *Le Peuple;* after Proudhon's death, published his works. In 1867 published his own doctrines as *L'Homme et la Revolution*. Though rich and living a retired life he joined the IWMA, and at the Basle Congress opposed Bakunin and contended for right of individual property. He was offered command of the National Guard in early days of the Commune, but refused it; joined the government in Versailles instead and wound up as a republican politician.

Leroy-Beaulieu (1842- ?). Political writer, author of treatises on female labor (1871), and on colonization. Contended that Marx plagiarized Proudhon, and that Capital, instead of exploiting labor, makes it more productive and thus better off.

Lorgeril, Hippolyte Louis, Viscomte de (1811-1888). Ultra-clerical royalist journalist, litterateur and politician.

Lullier, Charles E. (1838-1891). An alcoholic former soldier who was put in command of the National Guard by the Central Committee of the Commune, but soon arrested by it for being drunk and incompetent. In 1873 he was sentenced to death, but sent to New Caledonia instead; returned to France 1880 and became a Boulangist. Died in Panama.

Mulhouse. "The Manchester of France," in Alsace, and so lost in war of 1870; previously had had a third of all spindles in France. See note on Pouyer-Quertier.

Passy, Hippolyte (1793-1886). Finance minister to Louis Philippe and Louis

Napoleon; uncle of Frederic (b. 1822), economist and disarmament advocate.

Pouyer-Quertier, Auguste Thomas (1820-1891). Rouen mill owner; Thiers' finance minister in 1871; his handling of indemnity to Prussia is questioned as to enrichment of the Thiers gang and bribe for Prussian aid in "pacification" of Paris (see Marx, *Civil War in France*) As soon as Alsace was taken by Germany, he set up protective tariff against Mulhouse textile products. At public meeting following 1884 Guesdist conference, Lafargue raised this point and wrote Engels: "I drove them to fury when I told them that Pouyer-Quertier the cotton-master must have rejoiced at the signing of the surrender of Alsace, which relieved him of the competition of Mulhouse."

Reybaud, Louis (1799-1879). Publicist and politician; anti-Napoleon. In 1836 he published a lengthy study of socialists and other reformers.

Schneider, Eugene (1805-1875). One of an industrial dynasty that in 1837 set up at Creusot to build locomotives, and in 1874, as a "merchant of death," began manufacture of armorplate, gun metal, etc. His firm still exists, as Schneider SA, owners of electrical equipment manufacturers and other companies. The IWMA conducted a strike at his Creusot plant, shortly before the 1870 war, while Eugene Schneider was president of the Corps Legislatif. Since then members of the family have often misrepresented Creusot.

Simon, Jules (1814-1896) held chair of philosophy at the Sorbonne during reign of Louis Philippe; dismissed from this post by Napoleon III because of his open defiance of his seizure of power. In September 1870 he joined the Government of National Defense, urging a regime of order; included in Marx's denunciation of graft.

Thiers, Adolphe (1797-1877). Historian and journalist who supported the revolt of 1830 to replace Charles with Louis Philippe, aiming at a British-style monarchy to serve the business class. As Minister of the Interior in 1834 he suppressed the outlawed strike of silk workers at Lyons, but spread word in Paris that they had taken over the city thus bringing about a demonstration of leftists, whom he had slaughtered. Some think his 1871 plan followed the same pattern. As an historian he argued that a government defeats revolt most readily by surrendering the capital if necessary to remain mobile in the field, and then to besiege the rebels in the capital. President of the Republic 1871-77.

Tirard, Pierre Emmanuel (1827-1893). Thiers' handyman, mayor of the section of Paris occupied by banks and large businesses.

Villermé (1782-1863). Medical doctor and statistician; wrote on prison conditions and the condition of textile workers in 1840.

Paul Lafargue

The Charles H. Kerr Company Celebrates 125 Years---Then & Now!

Kari Lydersen

The world's oldest working-class and counter-cultural publishing house Charles H. Kerr Publishing Company was founded in Chicago in 1886, and continues to play a critical role in spreading information about labor struggles, civil rights, free speech and a wide range of dissident thought.

The Kerr Company has published numerous books by such luminary writers, thinkers, and activists as Upton Sinclair, Jane Addams, John Peter Altgeld, Florence Kelley, Jack London, Mary Marcy, Carl Sandburg, Clarence Darrow, Eugene Debs, Edward Bellamy, Claude McKay, Isadora Duncan, Vachel Lindsay, C.L.R. James, and Dave Dellinger. From Paul Lafargue's *The Right to Be Lazy* and Peter Kropotkin's *Appeal to the Young* to the first complete English edition of Marx's *Capital*, the company has issued many of the most crucial works in the canon of labor history, socialism, feminism, anarchism, surrealism, and other alternative literature. As Chicago labor activist Vicki Starr who starred in the documentary film *Union Maids* sums it up, "Charles H. Kerr is a publishing company like no other for their focus on books that other publishers do not, and will not, publish – books to help working people make this a better world."

The Kerr Company was started a few weeks before the infamous Haymarket police riot that resulted in the nation's first Red Scare and the execution of anarchist trade unionists who were prominent in the fight for the eight hour day. Charles Hope Kerr (1860-1944), the son of abolitionists, developed close ties to the Haymarket Defense Committee, the 1890's Populists, and later to the Socialist Party. In 1900, the firm started the *International Socialist Review*, the first major journal of Socialist theory in the United States. Because of the magazine's strong opposition to World War I, U.S. Postmaster General Albert Burleson put it out of business by denying it access to the mail in 1917. Throughout the years, the Kerr Company has always remained non-sectarian and open to various views of a freer and more egalitarian society. Its book list includes titles on Pan-African revolt, economic history, union organizing, animal rights, and the Mexican Revolution, as well as volumes of autobiography, labor action, songs, and radical cartoons.

Many of the Kerr Company's noted writers and supporters were members of the Industrial Workers of the World (IWW or Wobblies), formed in Chicago in 1905. Wobbly bard Joe Hill was especially close to the Kerr Company, which continues to publish books about him and his work to this day. Other vigorous supporters of the press included such outstanding wobblies as Vincent St. John, Big Bill Haywood, Elizabeth Gurley Flynn, Covington Hall, Irving Abrams, Sam Dolgoff, and Fred Thompson. President of the Kerr Board of Directors in the 90s, Carlos Cortez – well known for his linocut posters, murals, and poetry – was active in the IWW for nearly six decades.

In the '10's and early '20's, Kerr was the largest publisher of labor and socialist literature in the entire English speaking world. The repression that followed World War I brought hard times to organized labor, the Socialist Party, the IWW and the Kerr Company. The press' activity dwindled, though it did bring out several new titles by Clarence Darrow, and one of its all-time bestsellers, the classic *Autobiography of Mother Jones*, published in 1925.

From 1928, when Charles Kerr retired, through 1971, John Keracher and other members of the Proletarian Party, a small socialist group that concerned itself with workers' education ran the company. In 1971, IWW historian Fred Thompson, scholar of Native American medicine, Virgil Vogel, Sacco and Vanzetti Defense leader Joe Giganti, and several other labor movement agitators joined the Board and began reprinting some of the early Kerr classics. To honor the firm's centennial in 1986, more than 100 periodicals in the US. and Canada, as well as in France, Germany, Sweden, and Denmark, featured stories about the press. That same year, Chicago's Newberry Library acquired the Kerr archives – more than 60,000 documents, books, photos, and other items relating to socialist and labor history.

Now in its 125th year, the Kerr Company's current Board members include historian David Roediger, Milwaukee socialist Martin Ptacek, blues scholar Paul Garon, and Penelope Rosemont, longtime activist with the labor movement and the Chicago Surrealist Group.

Kerr continues to publish new editions of labor, socialist, and anarchist classics, as well as an impressive roster of original publications written and/or introduced by such accomplished scholars and activists as Robin Kelley, Staughton Lynd and Ron Sakolsky. Chicago rabble rouser and former City Councilmember Leon Despres introduced Clarence Darrow's *Crime and Criminals*; prison-abolitionist Gale Ahrens introduced a collection of, anarchist and Wobbly, Lucy Parson's writings and speeches, *Freedom, Equality & Solidarity*; and race scholar Noel Ignatiev introduced Wendell Phillips' *On Abolition & Strategy*.

Franklin Rosemont produced impressive titles, including *The Rise & Fall of the Dil Pickle: Jazz-Age Chicago's Wildest and Most Outrageous and Creative Hobohemian Nightspot*; and *Joe Hill: The IWW and the Making of a Workingclass Counterculture* – a comprehensive biography ("the best book ever written on Joe Hill," according to U. Utah Phillips). Paul Garon came out with *What's the Use of Walking if There's a Freight Train Going Your Way* that included a CD. The lavishly illustrated *Dancin' in the Streets*, by Franklin Rosemont and Charles Radcliffe tells the adventurous story of Chicago's younger Wobblies – also known as the "Left wing of the Beat Generation" in the 1960's. The book explores their magazine, the *Rebel Worker* ("the first revolutionary journal influenced by Bugs Bunny, the Incredible Hulk, and Harvey Kurtzman's Mad magazine."), the Roosevelt

University Free Speech Fight, the Solidarity Bookshop and Gallery Bugs Bunny, and the group's extensive interaction with anarchists, surrealists, situationists, Provos, and other far Left movements in Britain, Europe, and Japan.

For the 100th anniversary of the Wobblies' great free speech fight in Washington state, John Duda edited *Wanted: Men to Fill the Jails of Spokane*. Rosemont, Roediger, and Sal Salerno with great folklorist Archie Green edited the *Big Red Song Book* – the most interesting history of the IWW yet complied, one that combines its songs with its strikes, free speech fights and its resistance. Muhammad Ahmad (Max Stanford) contributed a book on his assessment of Black radical organizations between 1960-1975, *We Will Return in the Whirlwind*.

Not surprisingly, as Chicago's oldest publisher, Kerr has issued many books on Chicago and its history. Most of them – like the Bughouse Square Series – focus on the city's blue-collar counterculture and outstanding nonconformists. From the massive *Haymarket Scrapbook* to trade paperbacks like *From Bughouse Square to the Beat Generation: the Selected Ravings of Slim Brundage*, these books fill a gap that mainstream publishers ignore. As Studs Terkel, a longtime Kerr Company supporter, said: "We may be suffering from a national Alzheimer's disease, forgetful of what happened yesterday let alone years ago in our history. I suggest the perfect cure: Read the books published by Charles H. Kerr of old-time dissenters, muckraking journalists, and all-around noble troublemakers. You'll find these works an exhilarating tonic!"

As we enter the 21st Century, when organized labor and dissent are needed more than ever, its supporters expect the Kerr Company to keep going strong. There are plans, for instance, to reprint the *Haymarket Scrapbook* with AK Press and *Rebel Voices* with PM Press, to bring radical working-class history to a new generation.

Books from Charles H. Kerr

CPSIA information can be obtained
at www.ICGtesting.com
Printed in the USA
JSHW030304090722
27671JS00001B/9

9 781849 350860